THE SERPENT'S TONGUE

THE

Edited by NANCY WOOD

SERPENT'S TONGUE

PROSE, POETRY, and ART of

the NEW MEXICO PUEBLOS

DUTTON BOOKS ▼ NEW YORK

FOR KAREN LOTZ,

whose insight, patience, and love made this book possible

Published in the United States by Dutton Books,
a division of Penguin Books USA Inc.
375 Hudson Street
New York, New York 10014

Designed by Amy Berniker and Lilian Rosenstreich
Art direction by Sara Reynolds

Printed in Italy
First Edition
ISBN 0-525-45514-0
10 9 8 7 6 5 4 3 2 1

TITLE-PAGE ART:
Dancer with snake

ACKNOWLEDGMENTS

Hundreds of people contributed directly, or indirectly, to the completion of this book.

Karen Lotz, my editor at Dutton, first proposed the idea. She was born in New Mexico and perhaps has never gotten this magical state out of her system. My agent, Don Congdon, worked out the contractual details with his usual patience and good humor. My secretary, Magdalena Romero, worked for months to transcribe thousands of pages to the hard drive of my computer.

The rare-book sellers in Taos and Santa Fe were patient, kind, and helpful. They include Tal Luther, Art Bachrach, Riley Parker, Nick Potter, Judy Dwyer, and Jan Nelson. The two priceless Edward S. Curtis volumes on New Mexico were found in the collection of John Eugster in Aspen, Colorado.

At the Museum of New Mexico, Louise Stiver, Curator of Collections at the Laboratory of Anthropology, led me into the museum catacombs, where I spent hours poring over a collection of art slides, most of them never before reproduced. At the School of American Research, Dr. Douglas Schwartz provided support and direction; Mike Larkin and Christy Skinner gave me access to the SAR collections and made inexpensive duplicate slides. Pat Reck, director of the Indian Pueblo Cultural Center, introduced me to the wonders of that small museum and its stunning art collection. I also wish to thank Jenny James and Peggy Giltrow of the New Mexico State Library, Richard Rudisell and Arthur Olivas of the New Mexico Photographic Archives, and Orlando Romero of the New Mexico History Library.

For her support during this long and often difficult project, I'd like to thank my friend Virginia Westray. For his careful critical reading of the manuscript, his patience, and his tolerance of my mistakes and ignorance, I owe a debt of gratitude to Dr. David Warren of Santa Clara Pueblo. Ford Robbins, with infinite care and skill, completed much of the photographic-reproduction work. Andrea Waitt, Comfort Shields, and Jamie Michalak —editorial assistants at Dutton—were indispensable; we would never have made it through without their attention to detail, nor that of Andrea Mosbacher, Diane Giddis, and Suzanne Lander in the copy editing department. And to Sara Reynolds, Amy Berniker, Lilian Rosenstreich, and Semadar Megged, designers of this magnificent book, I'd like to express my deepest gratitude.

EDITOR'S NOTE

The Serpent's Tongue has its roots in Taos Pueblo, which I visited for the first time in 1961. I was struck by the magic of the land, the play of golden light on ancient adobe walls. The quiet dignity of the Indians impressed me. How had they survived? I read every book I could get my hands on. Soon I was invited often to the pueblo, where I acquired a different kind of knowledge.

Though not an Indian by blood, I recognized in the Pueblo Indians a profound strength and courage. As I read their history, I began to understand how, despite centuries of exploitation and inhumanity, they were able to survive. Rocks, trees, and rivers *do* live in them. Bears, coyotes, and eagles *do* guide them away from danger. Theirs is the Center Place.

So when Karen Lotz at Dutton Books asked me to do a collection of Pueblo Indian art and literature, I said yes. It was a chance for me to learn more; it was also an opportunity to present a wide range of material unknown to most readers. No anthology of Pueblo Indian literature had ever been attempted. How was I to proceed?

First of all, what is meant by *literature*? For me, literature is not only the marvelous Pueblo tales about creation, animals, and supernatural events but also the firsthand accounts of the conquistadores, who began their systematic destruction of a people and their culture in 1540. The Pueblo Oath of Office is literature. So, too, are traditional recipes and cures. Tales told for hundreds of years are included here. And many non–Indians also have their say: Frank Waters, Tony Hillerman, Willa Cather, Oliver La Farge, D. H. Lawrence, and Mary Austin all have written compelling accounts of a culture that they, like myself, can only know secondhand. Then there are the anthropologists—Frank Hamilton Cushing, Franz Boas, and Elsie Clews Parsons, for example—professional snoops who managed to extract some pretty good tales from the peoples they studied.

Most powerful of all are the statements by Indians themselves, and these include the great Acoma poet Simon J. Ortiz, Jemez historian Joe S. Sando, Laguna storyteller Leslie Marmon Silko, and Pulitzer Prize–winning Kiowa author N. Scott Momaday, who writes masterfully of his early days at Jemez Pueblo. At the Jemez

State Monument, built beside an old Spanish mission, I found heartwarming statements written by the Jemez Indians themselves, displayed as text panels at the exhibit. All of this was literature. And necessary.

For months I scoured the libraries and used-book stores. I contacted rare-book dealers and collectors. I purchased two rare and expensive books on the Pueblos of New Mexico (*The North American Indian*, volumes XVI and XVII) by Edward S. Curtis, which include not only 150 magnificent photogravures but comprehensive text found nowhere else. I discovered out-of-print volumes about such subjects as the fall of Pecos Pueblo; a book on how to bake one hundred kinds of Indian bread; tribal legends recorded and published by the Zuni people themselves; and a wonderful young-adult novel about the Anasazi culture, illustrated by the great sculptor Allan Houser. Tal Luther discovered an original unpublished line drawing by D. H. Lawrence of a Taos gourd dancer; he also

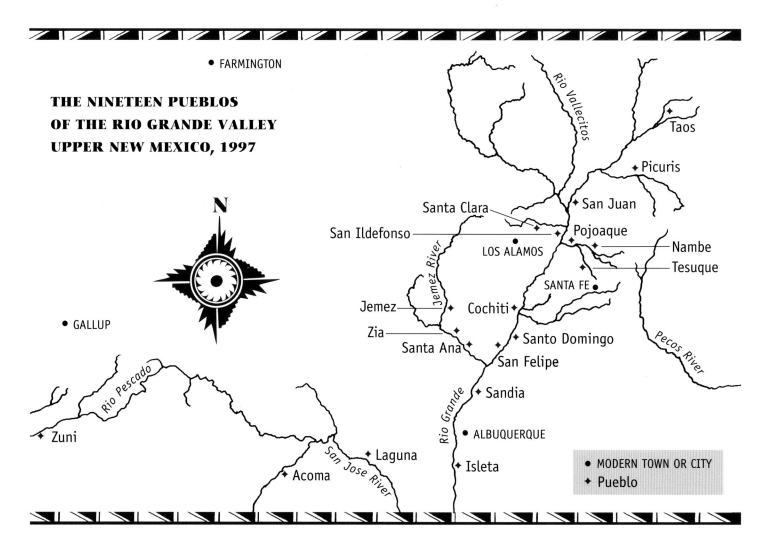

**THE NINETEEN PUEBLOS
OF THE RIO GRANDE VALLEY
UPPER NEW MEXICO, 1997**

N

• FARMINGTON

Rio Vallecitos

✦ Taos

✦ Picuris

✦ San Juan

Santa Clara

San Ildefonso

Pojoaque

LOS ALAMOS

Nambe

Tesuque

Jemez River

SANTA FE •

Jemez

Cochiti

• GALLUP

Zia

Santa Ana

Santo Domingo

Pecos River

San Felipe

Rio Grande

✦ Sandia

Rio Pescado

• ALBUQUERQUE

✦ Zuni

San Jose River

✦ Laguna

✦ Isleta

• MODERN TOWN OR CITY
✦ Pueblo

✦ Acoma

unearthed rather flowery accounts of Taos Pueblo life in periodicals going back as far as 1885.

In a used-book store in Santa Fe, I stumbled upon a huge portfolio of fifty full-color drawings by natives of San Ildefonso and Zia Pueblos. They are stunning examples of art done during the 1920s and '30s, when the Dorothy Dunn school became popular. (She taught Pueblo Indian art students to tap into their roots by producing simple, uncluttered paintings of tribal life and mythological subjects.) A number of these paintings are published for the first time here, including the painting of a water serpent on the front jacket of the book.

Trips to the Indian Pueblo Cultural Center, the Laboratory of Anthropology, the Museum of New Mexico, the Institute of American Indian Art, and the School of American Research yielded unexpected numbers of art slides, meticulously cataloged and captioned. The staffs of these places went out of their way to be helpful to me. At the end of the research phase, I had more than one thousand pages of text and nearly four hundred illustrations, enough for many books. Karen Lotz and I cut and revised during a four-day marathon editing session in Santa Fe. We not only selected on the basis of literary merit but also considered diversity, complexity, and originality. Either we loved a piece, or we didn't. The art struck us, or it didn't.

Readers will recognize, I hope, that this book is meant to be a tribute to a great native culture, a work painstakingly gathered and lovingly presented.

Nancy Wood
Santa Fe
1997

Endless testimonies . . . prove the mild and pacific temperament of the natives. . . . But our work was to exasperate, ravage, kill, mangle and destroy; small wonder, then, if they tried to kill one of us now and then. . . .

—Bartolomé de Las Casas, *History of the Indies*, Book Two (1548)

You might as well try to convert Jews without the Inquisition as Indians without soldiers.

—Captain–General and Governor don Diego de Vargas Santa Fe, New Mexico (1695)

Cliff-perched Acoma
(1904)
Edward S. Curtis

Historians have found the first treaty the United States government ever signed. It states that the Indians can keep their lands for "as long as the river runs clear, the buffalo roam, the grass grows tall"—or ninety days, whichever comes first.

—**Frank Marcus, Taos fire chief (1987)**

When mountains die, we die. When rivers run backward into time, our spirits will travel along. All is a circle within us. What ends here begins in some other place. What begins here has no end.

—**Traditional Tiwa prayer**

INTRODUCTION

In the Days of the Ancestors

The Pueblo Indians of New Mexico believe they came from a murky underworld, so long ago that the time cannot be measured in ordinary years. According to one of many legends, they knew neither death nor illness there, but they were not happy in such a dark and watery place.

One day they climbed up a spruce tree and emerged through the Shipapu, a sacred hole in the ground. The ancestors were sightless, so they turned toward the rising sun, and their eyes opened. They grew quickly into people of all ages, both male and female. A powerful spirit came with them from the underground, common to people and animals alike. Through this spirit, children learned how stars are connected to snakes, how trees are related to moths, and how rain comes from the Cloud People, the oldest ancestors. By imagining the underworld, the Shipapu, and the blind ancestors acquiring sight, people connected themselves to the spirit world.

This connection, this belief in the spirit world, was all the Pueblo Indians needed to survive. Tribes do not accept the idea that their ancestors crossed the Bering Strait land bridge and moved southward during the Ice Age. We have always been here, they insist. Our world came with us.

For countless generations, time stirred slowly under the hot New Mexico sun. Tribes moved from place to place, leaving few clues about their lives. Prehistoric memory evolved into tradition, which became the basis for legend and ritual. Pueblo religion stems from all of this, and more. Pueblo religion is life itself. Without it, the underworld would not have yielded the ancestors.

The Land and Its Lessons

The land of the Pueblos is magical. Crystal-clear light, olive-hued, plays across the vast red earth. Dark blue shadows dance long and changing paths. Mountains, covered with thick forests, rise toward a searing blue sky. On a clear day one can see a thousand square miles from a mountaintop. At night stars blaze across a black velvet sky. Sunsets, with their rich burst of magentas, ochers, oranges, and deep purples, are said to be the Sun Father dressing himself to go out.

Sunrise, according to legend, is when the Magpie Sisters part the Sky Curtain so the Sun Father can rise. Clouds form in the shapes of buffalo, coyotes, bears, eagles, sheep, and turtles. Our ancestors, the Indians say, are keeping watch over our people. To the west the desert shimmers with tantalizing mystery. Apache, Navajo, and Hopi live there. To the Pueblos, the land represents harmony between earth and sky. Their entire history belongs there. It is the Center Place.

Early on, the landscape and the people were one. It was their church, their cathedral. It was like a sacred building to them, but one without walls, tithes, or dogma. Nature had no need for sin, guilt, or redemption. Why should it? No Bible was necessary to mete out justice, form ties to the community, or force people to behave. The Indians knew right from wrong; they honored their elders, loved their children, and lived within a communal framework of work, cooperation, and tribal hierarchy. Prayer and observation were part of everyday life. Everything in the sky or on the earth was either male or female, because that was what the Old Man of the Sky and the Old Woman of the Earth taught them. If a man connected himself to the spirit of the land, he was said to be "living the right way." From the earth women learned about medicinal plants and herbs; earth provided food, shelter, clothing, and tools. The seasons reflected change, and women invented songs about their mystery. They watched men perform incredible feats based on superhuman physical strength and a holy alliance with their sacred land.

Serpent bird
Miguel Martinez

At Chaco Canyon, near Farmington, men carried from the distant mountains fifty thousand huge logs to build the town; they constructed four hundred miles of graded roads, the equivalent of four-lane highways. The ancestors knew about irrigation and crop rotation; they were masters of astronomy, architecture, plant science, and herbal medicine. But they did not invent the wheel or develop a written language. They had no need for them.

Something brought the life of these people, now known as the Anasazi, to an abrupt end—drought, disease, warfare, or a shift in religious power. By the mid-1300s most of the villages were abandoned, and the former residents moved to new sites along or near the Rio Grande. They left scant clues about themselves, but on the canyon walls they made pictures of animals, birds, mythical figures such as Kokopelli the flute player, clouds, corn, warriors, spirals, and other cryptic symbols of their lives. Archaeologists have spent their careers trying to learn what these drawings mean.

The Spanish Invasion

Many years before the Spaniards arrived, elders learned of them through Aztec traders, who reported the fall of Tenochtitlán and its great leader, Montezuma. Prophecies were told about A-wan-yu, the plumed serpent deity, who had retreated to the sky to prepare himself for the Time When Blood Flowed Alongside Water. Shamans took a solar or lunar eclipse to mean that drastic change was upon them. But despite the prophecies, the Pueblos were unprepared for what happened.

During the summer of 1540, the Indians of Hawikuh, today called Zuni Pueblo, were going about their timeless chores, singing as they worked, the smoke of countless fires wafting lazily into the clear blue air. They were unaware, until a lookout spotted them, that a column of soldiers in armor suits, riding splendid horses and carrying the twin banners of Spain and the Catholic Church, was marching northward toward them. By this time Hernán Cortés had wiped out the Aztec civilization in central Mexico, while in the swamps of Florida and Mississippi Hernando De Soto, with six hundred heavily armed troops and vicious war dogs, had slaughtered the native populations. De Soto's men, devout Catholics and trusted servants of the Spanish king, showed no mercy. (Nor had Christopher Columbus in 1492, when the peaceful Arawak, living on present-day

Haiti, failed to produce the required gold. He killed them by hanging, burning, unleashing his war dogs, or hacking off their hands so they bled to death.) Now the agrarian Pueblos were the target of religious and military fanaticism.

When the Hawikuh saw the Spanish troops approaching, they laid down a cornmeal line to indicate to them they were not to cross it. The Spaniards stormed the village, demanding gold, while an interpreter read the Requeri-miento, which had been written in Latin. This specious document, a joint procla-mation of church and state, set forth the uncompromising rules: henceforth the Hawikuh and their land, lives, and religion belonged to the Spanish king and to Holy Mother Church. If the Indians did not agree, the interpreter warned, "We shall forcefully enter your country and shall make war against you.. . . . We shall take you and your wives and your children and shall make slaves of them . . . and shall do you all the harm and damage that we can." The Hawikuh were puz-zled. They thought the Spaniards were gods—until twenty Hawikuh men were shot dead.

Next to be invaded by Spanish troops, with their powerful weapons and war dogs, were the twelve villages of Tiguex, near present-day Bernalillo. The village of Alcanfor was ordered vacated so Spanish troops could move into it for the winter. Men were forcibly stripped of their shirts, made of cotton and yucca fi-ber, in which strips of rabbit fur were twisted. The soldiers stole stores of corn, beans, and dried meat that the Indians had put away for the winter. One man complained that his wife had been raped. After the Indians killed a number of Spanish horses in retaliation, the conquistador Coronado sacked the villages. A forty-day battle ensued, after which two hundred Indians lay dead. A hundred others were burned at the stake. The villages fell to ruin.

Genocide began then, in 1541, in peaceful New Mexico. Blood dripped from the rooftops of Tiguex, and in the ashes of human fires only a blackened hand or twisted foot remained. Genocide in North, South, and Central America would continue for more than four centuries as native people, most of them unarmed, became the objects of greed and savagery by men who staunchly believed in a Christian God. As many as thirty million Indians were killed during those cen-turies––through warfare, disease, and starvation—by Spanish, English, French, Dutch, and American invaders.

At the time of the Spanish conquest, about twenty thousand Indians were living in seventy villages along the major river drainages of New Mexico. They spoke five mutually unintelligible dialects. Their lands stretched for thousands of square miles, across river valleys, mountains, and mesa tops. Coronado did not find gold in New Mexico, but there were thousands of souls to be converted, which meant that the Spanish king was eager to send both priests and colonists to that remote frontier. Forced to assist in their own "colonization" during the late sixteenth and seventeenth centuries, the Indians, usually women and children, built sturdy mission churches. Men grew crops and hunted game for their Spanish masters. With everyone busy making sure the Spaniards were fed, housed, and clothed, Indian families often went hungry themselves. Disease took its toll.

The Pueblo Revolt of 1680

For 140 years, from the time that Coronado left a bloody trail across New Mexico to the greatest Indian revolt in history, little changed in the pueblos. Indians were seen as pagans, beasts of burden, items of trade, commodities, savages, or animals, but never as men and women. In 1599, following a fierce mesa-top battle at Acoma, Don Juan de Oñate, the first territorial governor, cut off the left feet of rebel warriors. Countless more Acoma were put in chains and sold into slavery in Mexico. Eventually Oñate himself was removed from office in disgrace, but the Indians were demoralized.

The friars, no strangers to the whip, forced Catholicism on the pueblos. Those who refused baptism were routinely hanged; others were sold into slavery. Kivas were filled with sand and religious objects smashed. Medicine men were hanged in the plaza. Church and state fought over who had authority over the Indians; the state needed slaves, the church needed converts in order to justify Rome's outpouring of money into the far-flung frontier churches. The Indians survived this brutal period by pretending to accept the alien faith, but they practiced their own religion as well. Detection, they knew, meant certain death. Until well into the twentieth century, neither church nor state accepted the Indian religion. Kivas were raided as late as the 1920s. But when priests looked inside those native hearts, they saw something primordial and frightening.

Throughout much of the seventeenth century the pueblos seethed with resentment. There were numerous attempts at rebellion, but the powerful Spanish knew how to cure disobedience—with whip, noose, or sword. For generations, the Indians had dreamed of freedom. On Catholic feast days they sang about it in their own language, unfathomable to the Spaniards. Clan leaders from different tribes met secretly at trade fairs, wondering how to rid themselves of their hated masters. Their pueblos were scattered over thousands of square miles, and both civil and religious authorities watched their every move. The Indians called upon the spirits to help them. Leaders moved into the mountains to pray to their old, dependable gods.

A controversial San Juan medicine man named Popé masterminded a plan. Plotting for four years in the kivas of Taos, he devised a scheme of knotted yucca cords, one knot for each day, to be delivered by runners to each pueblo. When all the knots were untied, the Indians, from Taos to San Juan, from Acoma to Zuni and Hopi, would attack simultaneously on a given day. From a military standpoint, the plan seemed impossible. Distance alone was an insurmountable problem; so was the language barrier, the utter reliance on the runners. What else can we do? Popé asked. They had only to look at their decimated villages to know they could not last much longer. Many villages had perished during those 140 years. The irony was that the Golden Age of the Pueblos was over and nothing, not even revolt, could bring it back.

On August 10, 1680, the Pueblos struck in one great united effort over an area the size of Massachusetts. Four hundred soldiers and twenty-one priests were killed, though the Indians suffered a loss of three hundred warriors themselves. The great mission churches, built with Indian slave labor, were destroyed brick by brick; wooden statues, crucifixes, and altars were demolished. Many Indians ran to the river to wash the hated baptism from their souls; others scalped the fallen enemy and waved the scalps from poles. After a fierce battle at Santa Fe, where the Indians cut off the Spaniards' water supply to their stronghold inside the Palace of the Governors, the Spaniards surrendered. The Pueblos allowed them to leave peacefully, though they easily could have killed them all. The exit from Santa Fe ended in El Paso, on the Mexican border. The Indians burned the Spanish furniture and turned the Palace of the Governors into a pueblo, quartering their animals there, burying their dead, and installing baking ovens. This historic building is still standing; many believe that Indian spirits continue to live there. Every renovation turns up artifacts from that era.

Despite their common beliefs and origins, the Pueblo Indians were unable to live in harmony for very long. Popé, who had led the rebellion, insisted that the people give up everything Spanish, including the new crops and implements, and exacted his own tribute as dictator. Bitterness erupted, with each tribe reclaiming its former independence. Factions split into smaller factions. Greatly weakened by battle, hunger, drought, and smallpox, the Pueblos were easy prey for Comanche and Apache attacks. Leaders knew that without the Spaniards to protect them, life was almost as bad as it was under their former masters. When Don Diego de Vargas returned in 1693, many tribes bitterly fought the Spaniards as they had before, but, weakened and divided as they were, the Pueblos eventually succumbed. Vargas had come, he said, only to bring Christ to the natives, who were required to wear small wooden crosses around their necks.

In the eighteenth century the Pueblo Indians began to enjoy some of the things Spanish colonists brought along. Foremost was the horse, equal in value to two women. A splendid array of new crops—wheat, apples, peaches, pears, apricots, tomatoes, and chiles—added variety to the old diet of corn, beans, and squash. Cattle, oxen, donkeys, goats, pigs, sheep, and chickens eventually appeared in Indian villages. Metal tools such as hoes, shovels, knives, needles, and axes became indispensable. Gunpowder and European clothing and food also were introduced. The Pueblos learned the Spanish language in addition to their own dialects. The padres

Horse in the Wind
Ian Carlisle, age 11, Tewa

who baptized them gave them their own surnames—for instance, Martinez, Trujillo, Archuleta, Sánchez—which they retain to the present day, along with a number of secret Indian names. Intermarriage became more frequent, though the two cultures remain distinct and separate. Churches were painstakingly rebuilt. The Indians were known to put their own fetishes inside the thick adobe walls.

Swarms of colonists arrived; huge rancheros were established through land grants by the king, who assumed he now owned all the property that had belonged to the Indians and could dispense it to his friends.

Conquest, Change, and Conflict

In 1821, following the successful revolt of the Spanish colonists of Mexico against the Spanish crown, New Mexico became part of the Republic of Mexico. The opening of the Santa Fe Trail the following year provided a route by which Anglos could penetrate even more Pueblo country. Still, the Indians were little affected by any change in leadership until 1846, when New Mexico became part of the United States. As the new regime took over, rumors flourished about what would happen to Indians and Mexicans alike. They would lose all their land. They would have to report to the authorities. They would be forced to work for the Americans. One winter night in Taos, a group of angry Taos Indians and Mexicans rode into town and scalped Territorial Governor Charles Bent. More murders followed; then the Indians fled to the thick-walled mission church of San Geronimo at Taos Pueblo and hid there. A mostly volunteer army stormed the church with guns and howitzers; when fifty-one unarmed men tried to escape, the soldiers killed them. The army moved into the pueblo. Nearly two hundred Indian men, women, and children were killed; seventeen Taos leaders were hanged in the plaza. This was the last revolt of the Pueblo Indians, though the assault on their lives, lands, and religion was far from over.

After the American Civil War, opportunists, merchants, and settlers swarmed into the territory, demanding land for towns, ranches, and railroads. Unable to read or write English, many Indians simply scratched an **X** on a piece of paper and lost their land and water rights forever. They had no advocate within the government itself; the churches, far from actively seeking to defend Indian rights, offered salvation through Christ. The Indians turned to their old gods and prayed.

A generation later, the United States government began to remove Indian children from their homes and send them to boarding schools. Torn from their mothers' arms, the children were beaten, shut up in closets, forced to march to class to military music, and forbidden to speak their native languages or sing their old tribal songs. Their hair was cut short, their Indian clothing destroyed along with whatever sacred objects they might have brought with them. They were compelled to receive more Christian teachings from Protestant instructors. Some captives died in this hostile environment; others ran away; but most adapted, learning to read, write, and obey. After years of indoctrination, some students merged into the mainstream and never went home. Others returned and practiced their new skills. Many began to see education as a way of improving their lives. They became lawyers, teachers, skilled leaders, and craftspeople. Others took up an activist role. Though Indians were not granted the vote until 1948, many began to examine the legal documents that had deprived them of their land and water. They fought back with a different sort of weapon.

Victory

No symbol of Indian triumph over government injustice is more poignant than Taos Pueblo's struggle to regain their sacred Blue Lake. They believe they emerged from the underground via this lake and it is there the spirits reside, watching over them. High in a dense, unspoiled forest in the Sangre de Cristo Mountains, the lake is a pristine jewel, lying at eleven thousand feet. Every August the tribe goes there to celebrate its origins, to speak with the spirits, and to offer prayers of thanksgiving. To the Taos, Blue Lake is as sacred as St. Peter's Basilica is to Catholics.

It is not surprising that the government had long coveted this lake. Through executive fiat President Theodore Roosevelt made the lake and thirty thousand acres of Indian land part of the National Forest System in 1906. The Indians had not been told, and they became furious when they found their sacred lake closed to them, surrounded by a fence. The federal government issued grazing permits for sheep and cattle; they allowed hunting, camping, and fishing for non-Indians. The lake and surrounding area were quickly trashed; logging was planned, as well as mineral exploration. The Taos were allowed three days a year to use the lake themselves, and then only with the permission of the Forest Service. A legal battle, led by the Indians themselves, commenced.

After sixty-four years of relentless effort—lobbying Congress, blitzing newspapers, and a massive letter-writing appeal—the Taos forced Congress to return Blue Lake to them in 1970.

Not only was Blue Lake a symbolic victory for Indians pitted against an unsympathetic government, it had religious significance as well. After four hundred years of persecution, the Pueblos had proven, once and for all, their right to their sacred lands and rituals. They had defied the government through peaceful means and won. Federal officials would never again threaten to destroy the All Pueblo Indian Council, which had existed for centuries as a means to give common voice to Pueblo issues such as land, water, and religious rights. They would never again raid the kivas or drag children off to boarding schools. The Pueblos took charge of their lives.

Today, through profits from their gambling casinos, Indian leaders are pouring millions of dollars into education, housing, economic development, and visitors' centers. They effectively market their arts and crafts; the Indian Market, held every August in Santa Fe, is the biggest in the country. Indian writers have written movingly of their experiences growing up in the pueblos.

The connection to the ways of their ancestors remains strong in New Mexico's nineteen pueblos. When mountains die, we die, goes a Tiwa prayer. When rivers run backward into time, our spirits will travel along. All is a circle within us. What ends here begins in some other place. What begins here has no end.

CONTENTS

CREATION

THE ORIGIN OF THE MORNING STAR

There was once a woman living here in Zuni long ago, who had a child born which she thought was a real child, but which was really a canteen water-jar. When it grew up, it walked like a turtle. He saw the other boys go out hunting, and he wanted to go along too, but he couldn't kill anything.

And the Eagle (k'yak'yali) saw him one day, and said to himself, "Poor thing! He can't kill anything, I will kill for him." So he killed some rabbits for him, and the little fellow brought them home. And every time he went out, his friend Eagle hunted for him, and he always came home with meat.

When the snow melted away, he went down to the river every day, watched the other children play in the water, jumping up and down, and he wanted to play with them. At first he thought he wouldn't do it, but then decided that he might as well. So he jumped off a high place one day, and hit a hard spot and broke himself all to pieces. His mother came along and picked up the pieces, and brought them home and put them behind the fireplace.

Pretty soon the little broken water-jar said, "Mother!"

And she answered, "Yes, my child, are you all right now?"

And he said, "Yes, I am all right, but you must take the handles and the mouth of me and go out at daybreak and throw them to the east."

And she did as the little water-jar had told her, and took the handles and the mouth out early in the morning, threw them to the east, and they became the morning star.

Zuni tale, retold by Franz Boas

OPPOSITE:
Zuni Water Carriers (1903)
Edward S. Curtis

THE STARS

Many stars made bright holes in the clear, cold autumn sky. In the village plaza a fire danced and children danced around it. They were happy and excited because Old Father was in the village and would begin tonight to tell them the winter's stories.

"Tell us a story, tell us a story." They loved Old Father, and he loved them and understood them. His kindness made a warmth like the fire. He laughed and asked, "What kind of a story?" and a tiny voice came tumbling, "Why are some stars brighter than all the others? And why don't they ever fall where we can find them?"

The children settled around the fire as Old Father gazed up at the stars with a faraway smile. Pointing first toward Orion in the east, he said:

That is "Long Sash," the guide of our ancestors; he led our people to this beautiful land where we now live. Our people followed him without question, for he was a great warrior who had won many battles. He had grown tired of seeing misery all around him, his own people suffering because of the cruel ruler they had lived under for so many years. During his battles he had been in distant lands, and when he told his people about these places they asked him to take them there. They were determined to end their suffering by going away to a new land.

He tried to discourage them, telling them they had nothing to take along. He warned them of the hardships, the sickness, and the deaths they would face, but they were determined people, and in the end he could not refuse them.

They traveled with empty stomachs and scant clothing. Many died from hunger and disease, but they continued on and on. Long Sash taught them to hunt for their food, to make clothing from animal skins and bird feathers. After a time he led them into a land where no man, not even he, had been. It was daylight all the time, and they rested only when they were too weary to travel any more. Many children were born, and some died, but the brave spirit of these people kept them going.

Old Father paused to look around him. He saw all the children were gazing upward as if the stars, gleaming like mica, had hypnotized them. Waving his hand across the sky, Old Father raised the pitch of his voice, bringing the children out of their trance. They followed him, wide-eyed and open-mouthed.

"See that milky while belt across the middle of the sky?"

"Yes," they all answered at once.

"Well," continued Old Father, "that is the Endless Trail they were traveling on." In time, some of the people became doubtful and hard to reason with, and violence began to show itself here and there. Thereupon Long Sash decided that force was to be used on no one, that those who wished to follow him could come, and those who wanted to turn back could do so. In order to give everyone an opportunity to rest and make his own decision, he had them camp on the spot. It was time for many of the women to bear their babies.

Return from the Deer Hunt
Louis Naranjo
(photograph by Mark Nohl)

"See those two big bright stars (Gemini) to the north of Long Sash?" Old Father waited for an answer, but when none came he smiled and continued:

They are stars of decision. We must all make choices between forward or backward, good or bad. They mark the trail where Long Sash told his people, "If we choose to go forward, it will be a good choice, for the lives of the young stretch long before them. Choose the road back and you know what torture you will live. We have our signs ahead of us; let us not close our eyes, to see only the darkness!"

It did not take long for the people to decide to follow their leader. They all went on with lighter hearts and greater hopes. Long Sash sang

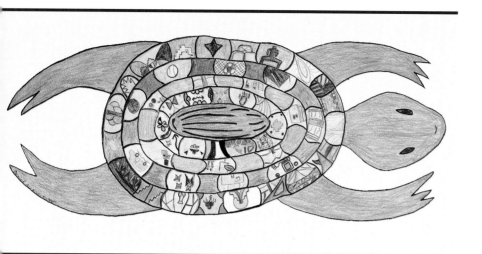

The Heart of Ohkay Owingeh
Daniel Archuleta, age 12, Tewa

loudly as he led his people on what seemed an endless journey. He hoped they would reach their destination soon, but he had prepared his people well, he had taught them patience, tolerance, and love for one another. Yet for some reason there was an emptiness in his own soul, and he could not understand the reason why.

He himself was growing tired of the long wandering, and when he was by himself he wept in despair. He began to feel strange beings around him and to hear unfamiliar voices. Not understanding these things, his first thought was that he must be losing his mind, but he was determined that he would lead his people to safety before anything happened to him. While he was resting he began talking aloud, and his people thought he was talking to them, and they gathered around him.

His voice was strange: "My fathers and my mothers, wherever you are, hear me, give me your guidance and give me strength to find our home. My people are tired now, and I am not young as I once was. Give me wisdom and strength to decide for them, and give me an omen, give me an omen!"

The people looked at each other fearfully, feeling the need for someone stronger than Long Sash to depend upon. They looked at him, who was now asleep. They discussed what he had said and wondered about the unseen beings with whom he had spoken. They became afraid of him, and when he awoke he sensed that something was troubling his people, so he gathered them about him and told them he had had a dream with many omens in it. He told them the most difficult part of their journey was over; traveling would be easier for the rest of the trip. He told them of the unseen beings and the voices he had sensed, and commanded that they be addressed as "Fathers and Mothers," and that the people ask for their aid whenever the need for help was felt. "Always have faith in them, for they will answer you with their blessings. I am not sick of mind. Now my mind is clearer than it has ever been. I will leave my headdress here as a symbol to all the others who may need a reminder of the greater spirits."

Old Father again pointed to the heavens toward the cluster of seven bright stars in the shape of a bonnet (Cancer) saying, "That represents the war bonnet of Long Sash." The children shifted a little and closed their mouths, dry by this time. He continued:

As they traveled they learned many new ways to carry loads. At first they bore their belongings on their backs, but now, with more babies to be carried, the younger men teamed up in pairs to drag the loads on poles. See the three stars (Leo) north of the headdress? They represent love, tolerance, and understanding, and were personified by two young men dragging their load and saving their people from worse hardship.

After a long time they came into darkness and everyone was afraid again, but their leader kept on, following a bright light coming through a very small opening (*sipapu* in Hopi; *sipo–pede* in Tewa). From somewhere they heard something digging and scratching. Still following the bright light they came closer to the noise, and when they reached the opening they found a little mole digging away. Long Sash thanked the small creature for helping them to find the opening, but the mole only replied, "Go, and when you again find my sign, you will have found your home." They found a cord hanging and climbed toward the opening.

Through the opening Long Sash saw Old Spider Woman, busy weaving, and he asked permission to enter. Replied Old Spider Woman, "You are welcome to pass through my house. Do not destroy anything and I will help you find your way out and show you the direction to take. When you see my sign again, you will have found your home." Long Sash thanked her, but he could not under–stand at the time what she meant.

Continuing on their way they came to a very cold, beautiful land to the north where they rested for many years. Some stayed to make their homes, for they were tired of moving. Long Sash told his people, "This is the land of ice and snow, and your helper is the bear, for he is big and powerful, as one must be in order to live here. Those who wish to continue I will lead, for we have not yet found any signs of the mole and spider."

The people asked Long Sash why he did not follow the sun to the west, and they went in the direction of the setting sun and came to a place where the land was hot and dry. They rested here for many years, some of them staying to make it their home.

Long Sash was restless, so he prepared to leave, saying, "This is the land of the coyote, the sun is hot and the air is dry, the wind echoes the wails of the creatures who live in the surrounding hills. It has its own beauty, but you who remain here will follow the ways of the coyote and wander about aimlessly preying on whatever you find on your way. Those who wish to follow me will go with me to the land of the sunrise where we will seek the sign of the spider and the mole."

Once more they traveled, this time until they reached the land to the east. There they found tall trees, plenty of water, and earth covered with green wherever they looked. Here indeed, they thought, was the land promised by the two prophetic creatures. Here life was easier, and many of the people were happy to make this their home, despite the ever present danger of wild beasts who often pounced upon them. The seasons were short.

Still they had not found the signs of the mole and spider, so Long Sash said to his people, "This is indeed a beautiful land where game is plentiful, but the seasons of warmth are short and the changes are too swift. This is the land of the cougar. He is dangerous and unpredictable as the seasons, so we will go to the south in search of the signs."

So, sad because brothers and sisters had parted, but with hope in their hearts and faith in their leader, they again set out until they came to a land in the south where the seasons were long, food was easier to find, and there was not the danger from lurking beasts. Still they were not sure this was their home, for they had not found the signs they were seeking, even though they searched all over the land of the south, to the borders of the lands of the bear, the coyote, and the cougar.

Long Sash called again for help from his spiritual ancestors, praying that they would again show him a sign. He felt low in spirit, but he taught his followers how to talk from their hearts, how to find happiness in their misery, and how to read signs. From him they learned a new way of life, guided by a new belief. Many of our ancient ceremonials born of that belief are still with us, but many others have passed with time.

After Long Sash's communication with the spirits of his forefathers, a great bird flew overhead and circled the pople four times before dropping two feathers from its tail. Falling to the ground, one feather pointed in the direction of the coyote, while the other pointed to the people. Long Sash then declared, "Here is our sign from our powerful messenger, the eagle. He tells us to follow in this direction!"

When they came to the new land, they found it to have seasons wet and dry, hot and cold, with good soil and bad. There was game, but it was hard to get. Here and there they found little scratches or tracks, but they had not found the mole as they had expected to do. However, close to the banks of a muddy river, they found an ugly little creature with a very rough skin and on his back a stone–like shell. He made the tracks of a mole, yet he was not a mole. Long Sash studied him for a long time before he exclaimed, "Look, he carries his home with him and rolls like a rock. He travels slowly, as we have done. On his back we can see plainly that he carries the sign of the spider; and when he moves, his feet make tracks like those of the mole."

This made the people very happy, for now they were certain they had found their homeland here where we are today. We move about a little now and then, but we will never leave this land, for this is where we belong.

The signs in the sky will always be there to guide us. Long Sash (Orion) is still up there leading many lost tribes over the Endless Trail (Milky Way). The Twins (Gemini), the two stars of decision, are choices we always have. There is the headdress (Cancer) of Long Sash, reminding us of his spiritual guidance; there is the team of young men dragging their load (Leo) to remind us of love, tolerance, and understanding. The big star (North Star) which guided our ancestors through the darkness is still there.

TAOS BEAVER TAIL ROAST

1 or 2 beaver tails
salt and pepper to taste

Broil tails over hot fire or under broiler until rough hide peels off easily. Roast tail meat in moderate oven until fork-tender. Delicious served with refried beans or garbanzo soup.

Phyllis Hughes

See those seven bright stars (Big Dipper) that form an animal with its tail hanging downward? That is Long Tail. Each star in this group represents a sign given us by one of the creatures I told you of, the mole, the spider, the bear, the coyote, the cougar, the eagle, and the turtle.

Look at the four high mountain peaks around you: to the north, Bear Mountain (Taos Mountains); to the west (Mt. Taylor), the Coyote; to the east (Sangre de

Cristo Mountains), the Cougar; and to the south, the Turtle (Sandia) Mountains. Within these boundaries our people found their home.

Why don't you find stars after they fall? Well, Long Sash is playing a game, and he catches them before they reach you!

The children sat and gazed upward, still hearing the voices of the past, as Old Father rose and stretched, saying, "I will pass here again, with other stories. Go home to your parents and sleep well. *Songe–de–ho*, goodbye!"

Pablita Velarde
Santa Clara
from *Old Father Storyteller*, Clear Light Publishers

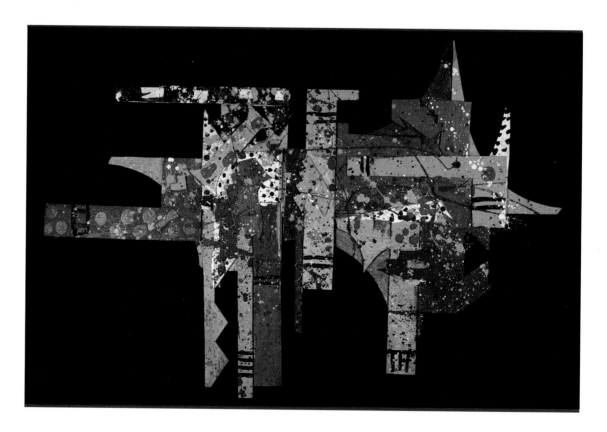

Coyote
Quincy Tafoya,
age 12

PART TWO

CHILDHOOD

THE UNBORN

"It seems—so the words of the grandfathers say—that in the Underworld long ago were many strange things and beings, even villages of men. But the people of those villages were unborn-made, like the ghosts of the dead. For as the dead are more finished of being than we are, they were less so; just as smoke, being hazy, is less fine than mist.

"And also, these people were, as you see, dead in a way, in that they had not yet begun to live, in the daylight fashion.

"And so, it would seem, partly like ourselves, they had bodies, and partly like the dead they had no bodies, for being unfinished they were unfixed. And whereas the dead are like the wind, and take form from within of their own wills (yan'te–tseman), these people were really like the smoke, taking form from without, from the outward touching things, even as growing and unripe grains and fruits do."

Frank Hamilton Cushing

Blessing of the
newborn
Harold Littlebird
Laguna/Santo
Domingo

PRAYER SPOKEN WHILE PRESENTING AN INFANT TO THE SUN

Now this is the day.
Our child,
Into the daylight
You will go out standing.
Preparing for your day
We have passed our days.
When all your days were at an end,
When eight days were past,
Our sun father
Went in to sit down at his sacred place.
And our night fathers,
Having come out standing to their sacred place,
Passing a blessed night.
Now this day,
Our fathers, Dawn priests,
Have come out standing to their sacred place,
Our sun father,
Having come out standing to his sacred place,
Our child, it is your day.
This day,
The flesh of the white corn, prayer meal,
To our sun father
This prayer meal we offer.

May your road be fulfilled.
Reaching to the road of your sun father,
When your road is fulfilled,
In your thoughts may we live,
May we be the ones whom your thoughts will
  embrace,
For this, on this day
To our sun father,
We offer prayer meal.
To this end:
May you help us all to finish our roads.

Zuni tale, retold by Margot Astrov

SONG FOR THE NEWBORN

To be sung by the one who first takes the child from its mother

Newborn, on the naked sand
Nakedly lay it.
Next to the earth mother,
That it may know her;
Having good thoughts of her, the food giver.

Newborn, we tenderly
In our arms take it,
Making good thoughts.
House–god, be entreated,
That it may grow from childhood to manhood,
Happy, contented;
Beautifully walking
The trail to old age.
Having good thoughts of the earth its mother,
That she may give it the fruits of her being.
Newborn, on the naked sand
Nakedly lay it.

Tewa tale, retold by Mary Austin

NEW MOON DAUGHTER

June 23, 1977

in the late night of a new moon you come forth
squirming and reaching, the color that is before dawn
entering from another world
quickly changing from blue to yellow to bright peach orange
and begin to breathe your new realm
a whimper from your tiny mouth then calmness
laying on your mother's belly, sucking on her breast
small body pulsing long and slow
child, you grasp with fragile hands and arms,
blessing us over and over
soon you will be presented to the sky and earth
your name will remind all of us who you are
sleep now, little one, sleep and dream for the people

Harold Littlebird
Laguna/Santo Domingo

THE LITTLE GIRL AND THE CRICKET

There was once a little girl who one morning went down to the fields to look at the corn and melon and beans. When she got to the field, she heard someone singing a song, and looked all around, but could not see anybody. It was Cricket (*k'etsiʟto*), singing in an ear of corn. She looked everywhere, but could not see who the singer was. Then Cricket jumped to another ear, and sang his song some more, and the girl looked around again.

Soon little Cricket looked out from under the ear of corn, and said, "What are you looking for?"

"I was looking to see who was singing," answered the girl.

"Why, that's me singing," said Cricket. "I'm singing because I am happy and in a field where there is everything growing."

Then the girl said, "Let's go up to my house, and you can stay with me."

"All right! I will go up and stay with you." So the girl took the little fellow up to her house, and he stayed with her all day.

When it was about bedtime, and they were sitting inside in a room, the girl said to Cricket, "Can you laugh?"

"No," he answered, "I can't laugh, but I can sing, just as you heard me in the garden this morning." So he sang a little more. Then he said to the girl. "You mustn't touch me or try to make me laugh, because, if you should touch me, I am so easily hurt that I might die." But the girl thought she would play a little with him, so she tried to tickle him; and he couldn't laugh, so he burst his stomach and died.

Tewa tale, retold by Franz Boas

THE SNAKE WHO ATE CHILDREN

Many hundreds of years ago, all of the pueblo Indians lived in a great communal pueblo which was on the Pecos River and was called Pecos Pueblo. It is now abandoned and in ruins. All of the people were perfectly content, making pottery, raising families, and farming along the fertile Pecos River valley. Due to the fact that they engaged in no warfare with one another and that the Plains Indians had not molested them for years, the population outgrew the living capacity of the farm, and there became a shortage of fields to feed so many people. The Pueblo Council of the Elders gathered in their kivas and discussed the various plans to remedy this alarming condition. One of the wisest elders came up with a plan: It would be best for all to continue to live together. He would take the first boy born in the pueblo after the meetings and, through his magic power, transform the child into a sacred snake. Another kiva would then be built for the home of the sacred snake.

Killing the serpent
José A. Martinez

From that time on, every firstborn child of every family would be fed to the sacred snake and the snake, by his magical powers, would provide for all the needs of the people.

All this was agreed upon and the snake was created. The kiva was built and the sacred snake was moved into his new kiva. Everything happened as was foretold and the people had plenty to eat and prospered and were happy. After the passing of many years, the snake grew to such an enormous size that it required more children than were originally agreed upon to satisfy its gluttonous appetite. The people dared not refuse the snake because he threatened to destroy their livelihood. The needs of the snake caused the population to decrease alarmingly and the people decided it seemed wise to get rid of the sacred snake. Such drastic measures were not to be taken lightly. So, one day all of the people gathered in the plaza beside the snake's kiva to decide what was best to be done. After much discussion, it was decided that the best solution would be to leave their mother pueblo, as they dared not stay with the snake. They would search for other homesites away from the snake. Many left the next day in panic and others soon followed. Some of them went across the mountains and started Nambe Pueblo. Others, following the Rio Grande, established many pueblos up and down its banks. Soon, Pecos Pueblo was deserted.

Legend says that the Cochiti group, one of the first to leave Pecos, settled in Frijoles Canyon and lived in cliff dwellings, and that these people are the ancestors of the present Cochiti Pueblo. The San Juan and Santa Clara groups started the Puye cliff dwellings and lived there until they moved down by the Rio Grande for better farming after a prolonged and severe drought.

The sacred snake had listened to all of this talk and heard the people leaving. He was remorseful, but also very angry, so

FEEDING THE SPIRITS

Before we eat whatever we grow, we feed the Spirit World. We have to let them have the first taste to express our gratitude. And for every meal that we eat after that, we have to feed the Spirit World first, and then we eat. Sometimes we forget, but then the old-timers remind us, because they always set the example at the table. They take a little pinch of the food and throw it to the four winds—so that the Spirit World will have the same food that we are having here on earth. And since the Spirits help to raise the food, it possesses great powers to heal the body and mind.

Pablita Velarde
Santa Clara
from *Southwest Indian Cookbook,*
edited by Marcia Keegan, Clear Light Publishers

during the night, he broke out of his kiva and hid. The next morning the remaining people of the pueblo trailed the serpent to a cavern that is now known as Pecos Cave. This cave has a small opening on the south side of Lake Peak in the Sangre de Cristo Mountains at an elevation of about twelve thousand feet. It has been said that the cave has been partially explored by local people who have gone into the interior of the cavern for about two miles at which point the cave is slashed by a deep chasm which they believe to be bottomless. The Indians say that this chasm was created by the tears of the snake while running away. Later, the tears dried up, leaving an impassable dry canyon. It is also believed that there is another opening to this cave on the north side of Lake Peak near Nambe Pueblo.

The Indians believe that the snake is still in the cave and it is said that every year, twelve Indian men from Nambe Pueblo go into the cave on the Nambe side and stay three days, and that only eleven men come out.

Tonita Peña
San Ildefonso

Tsle-ka (Douglas Spruce Leaf), Cacique of San Juan (1905)
Edward S. Curtis

THE GHOST

A fable used to frighten children into obedience

Long ago, when every one of the people lived here in one village, our children, who defied the authority of their elders, brought upon themselves the beings derived from the powers of the priests.

The children, young boys and girls, heeded nothing and continued their follies around the kiva in the center of the village. The priests warned them time and time again, but to no avail. Then when the priests had been tried and their tolerance exhausted, they gathered and discussed the situation.

The House Master, who belonged to a Kachina Clan, put forth his thoughts and announced what he was going to do. None of the other priests objected, so the House Master told them, "Starting tomorrow night, there will come a ghost and for the next three nights, it will continue to come." To one of the Bow Priests he instructed, "You will go out and inform your people. You will tell them of the ghost and that it is coming to make the people realize the value of their ancestors' ways. You will tell them that unless they start showing respect for their elders and the rituals of religious ceremonies, they, the people, will bring upon themselves destruction."

The priests discussed other things and shortly they left for their homes. The House Master entered another room where he began to prepare himself, then went on to eat the cornmeal. Finished, he went out of the village to the burial site of an uncle who had died at the hands of an enemy. Then he dug a small hole and laid in it the food he had brought along. As he did this, he prayed to his uncle, telling him of the plans.

A month later, from behind the place where the food had been placed, the uncle who had died came alive again. The ghost came directly to the little hole and through moans and weeping it ate all the food. Then when the ghost had finished, it spoke to the House Master. "What brought you here? Or have you something important to tell me?"

"Yes," answered the nephew, "I have something to say, I wish to please speak my part."

So the House Master of the priests told of the young children who kept up the uproar of noise, and said, "The children are making it very difficult for us to make a decision." He then talked about how everyone who had gone out to admonish them had been mocked, or at times even attacked with violent assaults; how, after much thought and consideration, the House Master thought he had come up with an idea that could solve their problems.

The ghost agreed to the plan, so they decided that four days later it would come upon the people in the village and for four nights would do as instructed.

The House Master returned to the kiva and informed the Bow Priests to call out to the villagers and inform them that the ghost would appear on the fourth night and that following that day, it would continue to come for the next three, in an effort to bring peace and quiet to the village. They were advised to feed upon the luxuries they had stored away for feasts and celebrations, because they might not have a chance to use what they had; they might not survive what was to be brought upon them.

The women immediately brought out from their well–hidden closet–type

The Demon of Childhood
Farny

chests large quantities of dried fruits, peaches, apricots, baked corn, and whatever else they had. They made stacks of tortillas with a meal of precious corn. Everything was cooked and prepared; for the next four days they ate very well.

When the day came, once more the Bow Priests went out and called to the people to use caution, for this ghost would surely come unlike anything they had ever seen or imagined. After the last meal, the village quieted, except for the young boys. Shortly after, the House Master had gone into the other room, where he ate some cornmeal and started out toward his uncle's grave site. There the ghost was prepared to come. After prayers, the ghost started for the village, while the House Master waited. Just outside the village, the ghost wailed hauntingly and chanted a song. Back at the grave site, the House Master heard an eerie shrill all over the village, and chills ran up and down his back. He declared himself that what was taking place was of his doing and that it was right, and so affirmed, he would not bring it to an end.

The ghost chanted the song four times as it progressed closer to the village, and the sound became louder as it came to the corrals, a short distance up from the river. The village was then in a tight cluster. The dark alleys that lay within the village went east and south from the main plaza. At that moment, a man had come out of his house and sat by the door, as the sun was bidding farewell to the world for the day. Then all at once the chant sounded. He sat there listening intently and heard the sound again.

The moon was shining brightly overhead, and the shadows began reflecting monstrous images. Another man came out, and the man sitting down declared he had heard weird noises. Directly, as if on cue, the sound came again. They stood in shock, numb with fright at the sound of the chant. Then the ghost appeared, and with it came a cloud of mist. The men remained motionless and silent, so the ghost went farther.

The ghost went back to the House Master's house, where it came to a stop for the night. The House Master came home, and in the dark and still of the night, he ate more cornmeal and then retired for the night.

Meanwhile, another man came along and found the two men in a state of shock. He started to try and awaken them, but it was useless. Finally the men regained consciousness and they told of what they had seen. From another direction, the sound of laughter from the group of boys near the plaza sounded loud and clear. The men, angered by this sudden outburst, approached them quickly and advised them to quiet down. They were only mocked by the boys and thrown from the booing group.

The three men decided to wait for the ghost until the next night and see if they could capture it. They left the crowd and went home. The next night, the men and a few boys from the crowd went out to where the ghost had appeared the previous night. They all held hands securely to prevent the departure of the ghost, but as it appeared, once more it sang the chant, and they all froze in their tracks, unable to either move or utter a sound.

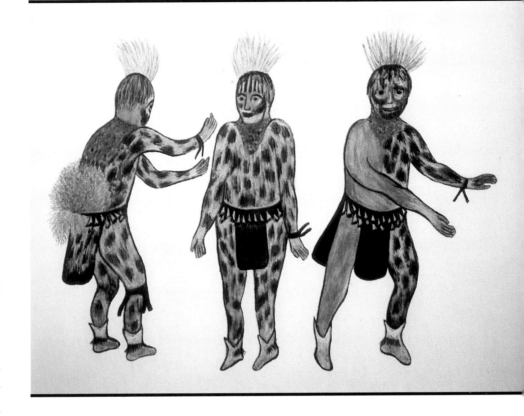

Santo Domingo Corn Dance (1930)
reproduction by Mary Alice Schively

The ghost reappeared and went through the line of defense, and along with it went the mysterious cloud. After a period of time, the men regained consciousness but were unable to comprehend what had happened. So twice the ghost had come and gone. Even though frightened, the men were sure they could apprehend the ghost the following night.

The next night the men separated into two groups, stationing themselves from one point of entry to the other. They assured each other that they themselves would not be scared after having already seen the ghost. So the men once more joined hands and waited as the ghost wailed the haunting song. As it did this it came closer. The men who had seen the ghost stood sure of themselves, while the others braced themselves against this horrible sight. The men stood ready and once more the torn, bloodied remnants of a man came upon them and went through the line of defense. The group at the departing point tried to keep the ghost from leaving, but it was of no use, for it could not be felt as it passed through their guarding line.

Defeated and anxious about their future, the men gathered and affirmed they would try their best to apprehend the ghost, for they believed that if they did not capture the ghost, their people and the village would be doomed.

On the fourth day the women and everyone else, scared to the point of hysteria, rushed about trying to keep themselves busy. Through the day, crying was heard in the village and some of the people sobbed at the thought of destruction, which they were sure would fall upon them within a short while.

As the sun began to set, the men formed a large gathering. They split up into groups to be at different points of the village, surrounding the area upon which the ghost had trod the night before. They instructed one another and soon were prepared. A short time later the ghost was heard, and once more the wailing of the chant began. As the chant faded away, the men clasped their hands and stood facing the entrance into the plaza.

The ghost came as though carried by a strong wind. The men standing there were pushed out of the way. Some clung to the rags covering the bloodied figure. As more men clung upon its rags, it was no longer able to lift itself, so the ghost came to the ground in the plaza. The men begged to be made known the reason for the ghost's appearance, and while the men threw questions upon the ghost, they heard the sounds of the young boys coming from inside the kiva. The men decided to bring the ghost upon the young boys, so it was led upon the roof of the kiva. Then the ghost was released, and it descended upon the boys, wailing as it approached them. The

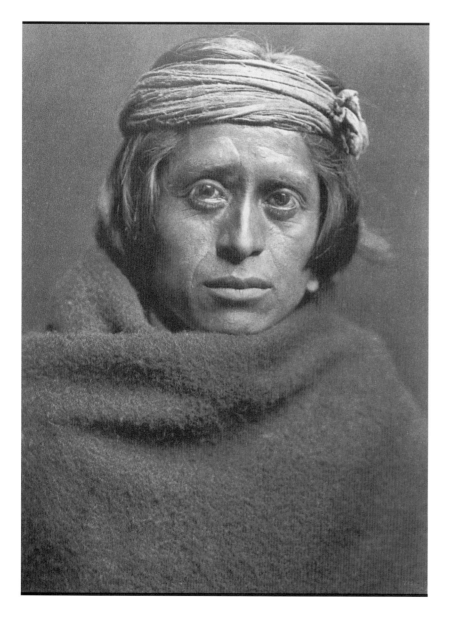

A Zuni Man (1903)
Edward S. Curtis

boys fainted from the shocking sight. As the ghost circled the kiva several times, the men entered and brought back the young men to consciousness, whereupon they began to cry and wail from fright.

The men pondered what they were to do with the ghost. Finally it was decided that it should be taken to the priest, where the purpose of its appearance would be clarified to them. The ghost was set before the priest and was then unclothed where they came upon it, dressed in the costumes of the four Kachinas. When the last mask was taken off, the face of the dead uncle was brought to light and it spoke.

"As each night our priests gathered to speak of important religious matters, they were interrupted by the noises and outbursts of the young boys. The people began to lose their sense of values and standards, which had dominated our lives, brought on to us by our ancestors. Tonight, of all the people here, you would have been doomed, but because of the blessings you received from our fathers, you have been delivered from an ill fate. But let no more of this improper conduct be continued. You will live in calm and order. But if you should persist toward the unwanted and undesired, there would be no alternative but for another of my kin to come upon you and there shall be no hope for you then."

The ghost was given prayersticks in offering and clothed with the Kachina mask, then it was led out of the kiva and proceeded back to the grave site where the House Master waited. The ghost, having done what was requested of it, clasped hands with the young man, and together they entered the grave, whereupon their spirits came to rest at Koh–thlou–wah–la–wah.

So, this was told to us by our grandfathers when we were growing up, and the fear of the ghost kept our village in order and also calm. But calm is not known to us any longer, for our young roam about at night and into the early morning hours, producing the most inconceivable sounds brought upon us by the advancement of times.

The Zuni people, translated by Alvina Quam

PUEBLO CHRISTMAS

It was dark and the moon had gone behind a cloud. The air was cold as Uncle Narcisus and Rabbit left Grandfather's house early Christmas morning.

Rabbit had put on the long wool dancing stockings. He wrapped his feet with wool wrappings before he put on his moccasins. Now he and his uncle were wrapped in heavy wool blankets. They were very quiet as they left the house. Then they went to the mesa south of the village. There was a large fire made of cedar wood. It was the place where all the little boys who would be antelopes met to prepare for the dance.

They could not see over to the east mesa, but they knew the young men and one young woman were getting ready. They would be the two buffalo dancers, the buffalo girl, and also, all the deer and big horn sheep dancers. Everyone had been practicing for two weeks. Now was the big day!

Rabbit and his uncle approached the fire. They opened their blankets to catch the heat and warmed themselves.

"It is time to finish your costume," said Uncle, as he spread the large sheet of cloth that had been designed to look like an antelope skin. It was painted to show that the antelope had a tan color with a white belly and rump. A real antelope's tail was sewn in the back. Now this was placed on Rabbit and fastened in the front, under his arms, and around his legs. Uncle took some dark coloring and painted Rabbit's face. Then he pulled the top over his head and fastened it under his chin. He sprayed Rabbit's face with sticky, wet liquid. Uncle sprinkled mica flakes and this made his face shine in the firelight.

"Stand up straight so I can put your headdress and feather cape on you," said his uncle. Rabbit had been jumping up and down trying to keep warm.

Uncle placed a pair of antelope horns and ears on his head and tied them with the leather strap. A cape of red hawk feathers was attached behind his horns and a visor shield of yucca leaves in the front. Now red and green yarn ties and sleigh bells were placed on his legs just below his knees. Bands were put around his arms. Then his uncle handed him a stick which was decorated with turkey feathers. This had a padded ball on one end. Rabbit would lean on this stick as he danced.

Rabbit noticed the first light of dawn. The shadows made by the fire disappeared. Uncle Narcisus picked up his blanket and the sack which had contained Rabbit's costume. He turned to Rabbit, put his arms around him and blessed him.

"You are a fine looking antelope," he added. "I know you will make us proud because the elders have chosen you as the leader of the antelopes."

"I will do my best to bring honor to our family, my uncle," replied Rabbit.

Rabbit's uncle and the men who had dressed the other antelopes now looked to the mesa where the buffalo dancers were. They saw a large white cloud of smoke rising from the east mesa. The little antelopes dashed here and there to keep warm. They jumped over rocks and tree stumps. They laughed and yelled in the frosty morning.

The drums and the singers could be heard clearly in the distance. The white smoke was the signal that the buffalo dancers would begin their walk down the side of the mesa and into the village.

"Young men of the antelope, calm down and gather around me. This is the dawning of another Christmas day. We must pray before we go to join the buffalo and meet our pueblo elders," said one of the tribal leaders.

Bear carrying dead deer
Awa Tsireh

Rabbit and the others gathered around, as the leader solemnly said a prayer. Then he gave each antelope the blessing of the Great Spirit.

All the antelope lined up behind Rabbit. Then they ran down the side of the mesa, being careful to miss the rocks and cactus. Rabbit was excited as the cold air hit his face. He could feel his hawk feathers blowing behind his head.

They reached the trail to the village; Rabbit signaled them to stop. They formed a circle. Each leaned on his stick which they placed in front of themselves, one hand over

the other. They looked at each other to see if their costumes were still together after the fast run down the hill.

Rabbit noticed the buffalo dancers were crossing the wagon road. Now was the time to start towards them.

"Let's go," said Rabbit. The others followed in a line. Rabbit could hear the thud of their moccasins on the frozen ground.

As the buffalo dancers reached the first of the line pueblo leaders at the edge of the village, the antelope dashed into sight. The deer and the big horn sheep dancers followed the buffalo dancers. Rabbit stopped the antelope a short distance away. They again formed a circle to wait. All the dancers walked by the line of men wrapped in blankets and received their blessing.

The drummers were playing a slow dance song by the time the last antelope passed through the line of elders. Now they raced between the houses and into the plaza. They arrived beside the drummer just in time to join the others in a fast dance.

Now Rabbit listened to his clan's drums all that day. When he heard his drums begin to play, his group of antelope joined him. They would run all over the village. They ran between houses and tumbled–down adobe. They ran on the roof tops and along the plaza. When the drums began a fast dance, they would stop right where they were. They formed a circle with their hands on their sticks and they danced.

Once they ran down a back street. A village dog came after them. All the antelope turned and chased the dog with their sticks. The boys laughed as the dog went howling away. They returned to their dancing.

The dancing and fun continued all Christmas Day. At sundown some men of the village walked up and down the plaza carrying guns. Rabbit led his group of antelope into the plaza. Then the men shot their rifles into the air. All the antelope, deer, and big horn sheep dropped to the ground as if they had been shot. They lay very quietly until each hunter picked one of them up and carried him to his own house.

The sun was now behind the red mesa in the west. Another Christmas Day had ended.

Lawrence Jonathan Vallo
Jemez/Acoma
from *Tales of a Pueblo Boy*, Sunstone Press

BABY EAGLES

Snow was going from the valley. The stately old cottonwood trees were giddy girls again, flaunting the fresh new buds of spring. At dawn, when the old man and the young boy went to the edge of Zuni to watch the shadows the sun made in its journey across the sky and around the year, it was now not so cold.

Grandfather told his little son about the Rain Makers. Rain Makers are the shadow people. Their work is to gather drops of water into gourd jars from the six great waters of the world. These shadow people are so sacred that the earth people must never see them. So the gods make clouds with their breath that the Rain Makers may hide behind them. The Rain Makers pour their drops of water through these cloud masks onto the thirsty men and the thirsty fields below.

Swallows bring the rain. Zuni say, "Swallows sing for rain." Grandfather sang the swallow song for Ze-do. It is such a little song.

> *Hitherward! Hitherward!*
> *Rain clouds.*
> *Hitherward! Hitherward!*
> *White clouds.*
> *He yai–e lu.*

One day all the fathers of Zuni met in the plaza. They had their little boys with them. Grandfather said that they were going eagle catching. For the first time Ze-do was sorry that he was growing to be a big boy. For the first time he wished he could be little. At least, for the day of eagle catching.

All the fathers and their little boys and their grandfathers and Ze-do and his

ACOMA AND LAGUNA CALENDAR

April (Sticky ground; wheat sowing time),
    Pus-chuts-otes
May (Ground soft like ashes; corn planting),
    Sho-wats-otes
June (Corn tassel), A-chin
July (First appearance of corn ear), Hi-shin
August (Beard of the corn), Ya-mon
September (Corn in the milk), Ki-nut
October (Mature corn), Ki-ti-stchi-ta-ta
November (Fall of the year), Hai-a-tassi
December (Middle of the winter), Sin-ni-kok
January (Moon when the little lizard's tail freezes
    off), Me-yo sitch ta-watch
February (Plant root; daughter of spring), Yu-mun
March (Same plant above ground), Stchum-mu

                    Hamilton A. Tyler

Grandfather went across the river and along the sandy trail that led up to Sacred Mountain. The fathers had coils of ropes and baskets underneath their blankets. The little boys had fast–beating hearts underneath their blankets. It takes a strong boy, and a brave one, to catch an eagle, even though it is a baby eagle.

After a long climb they reached the sharp peaks of Sacred Mountain. The great plain of Zuni looked far below them. The high houses of Zuni looked little. Ze–do remembered the blocks that the tiny children played with at school. The Zuni houses from the peaks of Sacred Mountain looked like rows of these little blocks.

Now a father was looking over the rock side. He was looking for a ledge on the cliff face for there the eagles built their nests.

All at once Ze–do gave a high cry. He was looking through a crack of rock, down, down, down. Grandfather came to stand beside him. Yes, there far below them on a narrow shelf of rock was an eagle's nest with baby eagles in it.

The men crowded to the crack. They looked down. "Yes, yes," they said, "it is an eagle's nest." The men looked up into the blue above them. No angry mother eagle soared above her babies.

Quickly one of the men seized his little boy. Quickly he tied a rope about the child's waist, and swung him over the side of the rock cliff. Slowly, slowly, the little boy swung in a circle; his small hands held tightly to the tope going upward to his father's sure hold.

Anxiously, all the men looked down at the slowly swinging boy. Anxiously, they looked up at the empty sky. If the mother eagle should return she would attack the little boy, far down there swinging from the rope his father held.

Ze–do's breath came fast and sharp. He felt that he could not wait until the boy on the rope had captured his bird and was pulled up to safety.

At last the little boy's feet stood solidly on the rock ledge. He took his hands from the rope, and walked the few steps to the eagle next. He looked in, then, quickly, he grabbed a baby bird and the men began to pull on the rope. Only one hand held to the rope now. The other held the eagle baby captive within his shirt.

The small body dangling from the rope end rose steadily and swiftly. Now many men were at the rope, pulling, pulling, for far, far against the sky clouds could be seen the mother eagle flying in furious flight to protect her young.

When the little boy was safely among the men again, Ze–do brought the wicker cage and helped put the captive eagle in it.

He went to another rock point and searched in all crevices there and tried to be the first again to find another nest.

As each little boy went over the side of the rock cliff, Ze–do felt as if it were himself. He could feel himself swinging with the little boy, down, down, down. He could feel himself snatching the baby eagle and being pulled up, up, up, along with the little boy. Ze–do felt like the fathers when they were lowering their little boys and bringing them up again to safety.

It was a great day. Many baby eagles were captured. The fathers put the baby birds in willow cages to carry down the trail to the pueblo. The cages would be the home for the babies, now. Some of the boys insisted that they carry their own eagles down the trail. Others were glad for their fathers to help them.

Some of the old men were remembering other eagle–catching days. They were telling stories about them. Ze–do walked with them. He felt grown up, now that he was too large to do things with the little boys. He said to one of the old men, "Those children did better than I thought they could do." The old man did not even look at him as he answered, "Yes, we men forget how strong the children are."

Ze–do liked this answer very much. He said to himself, "I must say those words to my grandfather when he and I are talking about the eagle catching."

The way home seemed very long. It was cold, too, after the sun went away. Stars lighted the sky, and candles lighted the windows of the houses of Zuni. When the men and the little boys and the captive eagles reached the plaza, the house doors opened to ask them to warmth and bed. When Ze–do and Grandfather reached their house, Quatsia had fire and supper waiting for them.

Ze–do told Quatsia, "We had a fine day, but I was never so tired before in all my life. When I eat my supper I am going to bed."

He had forgotten all about the words the old man had said to him, coming down the trail from Sacred Mountain. He had forgotten that he was going to say to his Grandfather, "We men forget how strong the children are."

Zuni tale, retold by Ann Nolan Clark

A TRICK

There was this old man
and he had a wagon.
One of those with large wheels in the rear
and small ones in front.

In those days
the people would get up
early in the morning.

Especially if they were going somewhere,
to the mountains after wood,
across the river to the fields,
some far place.
It would still be dark.
Well, I guess some young men
or somebody
wanted to play a joke on this man.
So they changed his wheels around,
the large ones to the front,
the small to the rear.

He stopped three times
trying to figure out what was wrong.
Later,
he said,
"I keep feeling like I'm going up a hill."

After that,
the young men
weren't allowed out
around the village at night
as much as before.

Larry Littlebird
Laguna/Santo Domingo

Okuwa-T'sire (Cloud Bird),
San Ildefonso (1905)
Edward S. Curtis

HAVE YOU EVER HURT ABOUT BASKETS?

Have you ever hurt about baskets? I have, seeing my grandmother weaving for a long time.

Have you ever hurt about work? I have, because my father works too hard and he tells how he works.

Have you ever hurt about cattle? I have, because my grandfather has been working on the cattle for a long time.

Have you ever hurt about school? I have, because I have learned lots of words from school, and they are not my words.

Marylita Altaka
Pueblo schoolchild, 1970

CIRCLE OF WONDER

I was a boy of twelve when my parents and I moved to Jemez Pueblo, New Mexico, in 1946. There was a village of a thousand people, three telephones, two windmills, three or four pickups and no automobiles. But there were horses and wagons. There were cornfields and orchards, there were beehive ovens and brilliant strings of chiles, and there was an ancient architecture that proceeded immediately from the earth. There was an immense and incomparable landscape, full of light and color. And there were people of great dignity and good will and generosity of spirit. It was a place of singular beauty and wonder and delight.

My first Christmas there was beyond my imagining. On Christmas Eve the bonfires were lighted, and sparks rose among the stars. The air was cold and crisp and scented with sweet smoke. The night sky was radiant; the silence was vast and serene. In all the years of my life I have not gone farther into the universe. I have not known better the essence of peace and the sense of eternity. I have come no closer to the understanding of the most holy.

N. Scott Momaday
Kiowa
from *Circle of Wonder*, Clear Light Publishers

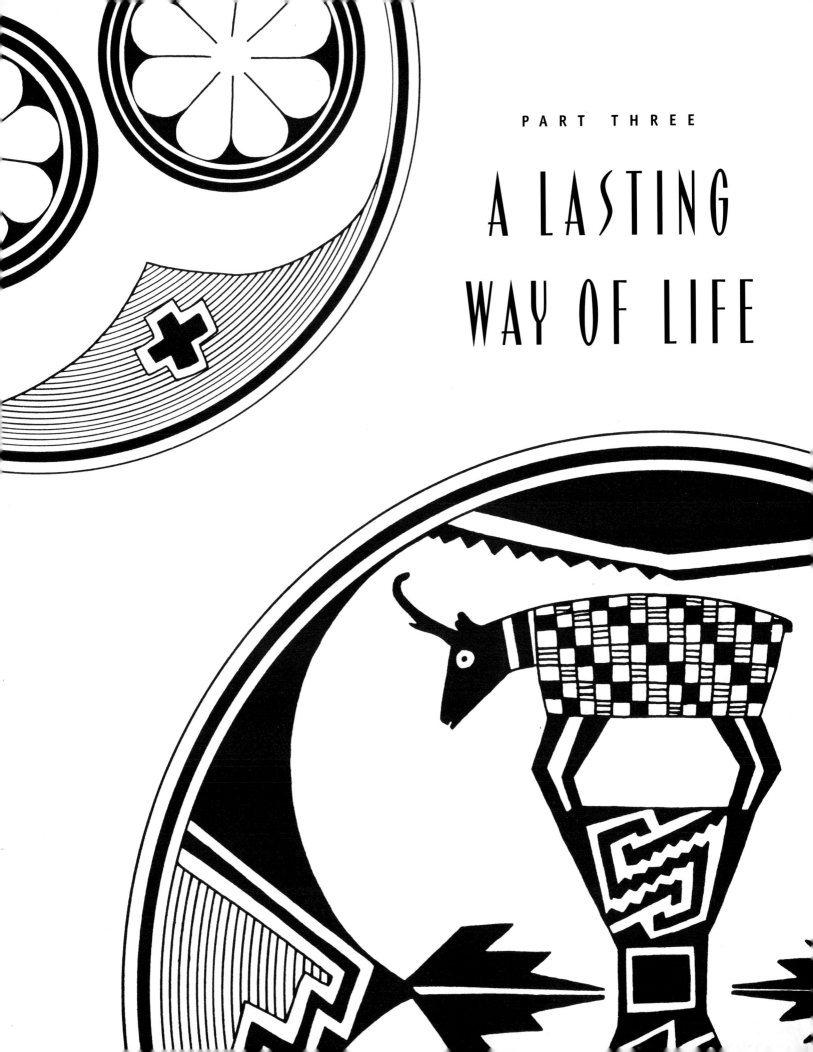

PART THREE

A LASTING
WAY OF LIFE

INSTRUCTIONS ON LIFE

In the beginning were the Instructions. We were to have compassion for one another, to live and work together, to depend on each other for support. We were told we were all related and interconnected with each other.

Now people call our Instructions legends because they were given as stories. But to the Indian people, that was like a reality at some point in history. So most of the Indian nations that we know of, they have their own story of where they began. Some will tell you they came from the sky, from the stars. Some will say they emerged from the earth or they emerged from a lake as a people. In that emerging, it's almost like they were choosing their language, choosing dress style, songs, their dances.

So that was the beginning.

The Instructions during that time, at the beginning, were to love and respect one another even with all the differences—different cultures, different languages.

We were told we were all from the same source. We were coming from the same mother, same parents. The Instructions were to help us live in a good way and be respectful to everybody and everything. We were told if the Instructions were lost, then harm would come to the people.

In the beginning we were given our Instructions of how to live. So that's been handed down from generations to generations until now. "This is how to live."

Vickie Downey
Tewa/Tesuque

A VAST OLD RELIGION

A vast old religion which once swayed the earth lingers in unbroken practice there in New Mexico, older, perhaps, than anything in the world save Australian aboriginal taboo and totem, and that is not yet religion. You can feel it, the atmosphere of it, around the pueblos...

But never shall I forget watching the dancers, the men with the fox-skin swaying down from their buttocks, file out at San Geronimo, and the women with seed rattles following. But never shall I forget the utter absorption of the dance, so quiet, so steadily, timelessly rhythmic, and silent, with the ceaseless downtread, always to the earth's centre ... Never shall I forget the deep singing of the men at the drum, swelling and sinking, the deepest sound I have heard in all my life, deeper than thunder, deeper than the sound of the Pacific Ocean ... the wonderful deep sound of men calling to the unspeakable depths ...

Pueblo Indian Dancers
D. H. Lawrence

It was a vast old religion, greater than anything we know: more starkly and nakedly religious. There is no God, no conception of a god. All is god. But it is not the pantheism we are accustomed to, which expresses itself as "God is everywhere, God is in everything." In the oldest religion, everything was alive, not supernaturally but naturally alive. There were only deeper and deeper streams of life, vibrations of life more and more vast. So rocks were alive, but a mountain had a deeper, vaster life than a rock, and it was much harder for a man to bring his spirit, or his energy, into contact with the life of the mountain, and so draw strength from the mountain, as from a great standing well of life, than it was to come into contact with a rock. And he had to put forth a great religious effort. For the whole life-effort of man was to get his life into direct contact with the elemental life of the cosmos, mountain-life, cloud-life, thunder-life, air-life, earth-life, sun-life. To come into immediate *felt* contact, and so derive energy, power, and a dark sort of joy. This effort into sheer naked contact, *without an intermediary or mediator,* is the root meaning of religion, and at the sacred races the runners hurled themselves in a terrible cumulative effort, through the air, to come at last into naked contact with the very life of air, which is the life of the clouds, and so of the rain . . .

It was a vast and pure religion, without idols or images, even mental ones. It is the oldest religion, a cosmic religion the same for all peoples, not broken up into specific gods or saviours or systems. It is the religion which precedes the god-concept, and it is therefore greater and deeper than any god-religion.

D. H. Lawrence

PUEBLO INDIAN RELIGION

The Pueblos have no word that translates as "religion." The knowledge of a spiritual life is part of the person twenty-four hours a day, every day of the year. In describing the beliefs and practices of today, the traditional religion may also be understood. There is little basic change. The tradition of religious belief permeates every aspect of the people's life; it determines man's relation with the natural world and with his fellow man. Its basic concern is continuity of a harmonious relationship with the world in which man lives. To maintain such a relationship between the people and the spiritual world, various societies exist, with particular responsibilities for weather, fertility, curing, hunting, and pleasure or entertainment. Even today, most Pueblo people belong to a religious society, and have an important place in the Pueblo, with time set aside on the Pueblo calendar of religious events. The calendar is so full that there is no time left for any new or innovative religious practices, as is sometimes possible with non-Pueblo Indians who accept, as one example, the Peyote Way. Many tribes that espouse new religions which are a combination of the old with the new beliefs, suffered various defeats, had lost their land to white invaders, and lost a great part of their culture as well. Certainly they could not remove their sacred artifacts nor their religious shrines at the point of a bayonet. Thus they had to revive their religion in a new homeland.

But the Pueblos are still living today upon the sites where the Spaniards found them in the 16th century. This is the principal reason for their religion being practically intact. The people took their religion underground around 1692, due to harassment by the Spaniards in their attempt to substitute another religion for the native one. This fear still persists, and it generally explains why a non-Indian is not permitted to observe a religious ceremonial dance in the Pueblos, and why no cameras or sketching are allowed.

The religious rituals and ceremonials themselves, maintained by the Pueblos today, are the same they have practiced since their ancestors lived in pit houses. The oratories, prayers and songs are the same. These observances are not spontaneous outpourings, or outbursts of the troubled heart. They are carefully memorized prayerful requests for an orderly life, rain, good crops, plentiful game, pleasant days, and protection from the violence and the vicissitudes of nature. To appease or pledge their faith to God, they often went on sacrificial retreats, often doing without food and water as penance or cleansing of body and soul for the benefit of man throughout the world.

Joe S. Sando
Jemez

Runaway Koshare
José Rey Toledo

ALL AS IT WAS IN THIS PLACE TIMELESS

All as it was in this place timeless.
All as it was between the human soul and the earth
For there is no difference between
The life of a man and the life
Of all growing things.
Who is to say if a man
Shall not be a tree instead?
We pray to all of nature and do it no harm.
These are our brothers
All men and all animals and all trees.
Some part of ourselves
Is in earth and sky and everywhere.
It shall continue
As long as nature follows its own purpose.
It shall continue
As long as we know what we are doing here.

Nancy Wood

Five Brothers
**Jordan Harvier,
age 12, Tewa**

A CIRCLE BEGINS

in the surround of snow–touched mountains
a circle begins
in a meadow by a snow melt creek
where hands weave a house of thin green saplings
it is a way of song
a way of breathing
a pure womb to center oneself through sweat
a way of blessing and being blessed
a circle of humility, prayer and asking
and there are no clocks to measure time
but the beating of our singing hearts

Harold Littlebird
Laguna/Santo Domingo

CALAVERA DE PERRO
(DOG SKULL)

Calavera de perro is considered as a recognized remedy for sprained joints or in healing broken bones. You first locate an old dog skull. The skull is then ground into a fine powder. The next step is to heat the powder in the oven until it turns brownish in color. The powder is then applied with grease to the area of the sprained or broken bone, after the bone has been set. A splint is then applied, and in the course of time you will find that the bone is healed without any resulting difficulties.

Tibo J. Chavez

GOING TO BLUE LAKE

Days grew long and hot and lazy. Little boys shouted and played on the rooftops of the houses. They played along the narrow passage-ways between the houses. They played in the hidden patio gardens. Grandfathers made them bows and arrows and rabbit sticks and little drums. They taught them songs and dance steps. They told them stories.

Father brought home two new, white sheets. One was large and one was small. Father put the large one on, wrapping it about his hips, folding it in wide, neat folds. Tso'u put the small one on, twisting himself about to see if he looked like a real man. He did. At least he thought he did.

Father sat down on the wall-ledge seat. He stood his small boy between his knees and talked to him of many things that boys should know. He told his son about the work of growing up to be a man. He told his son how a man's trail through life should go. He said, "A man must keep his footsteps in the trail that he has chosen."

He told the boy about Taos sacred lake. How the mountains held and hid it. How the snows of winter fed it. How the sky leaned tenderly over it and gave blue color to its still, deep waters. With a stick Father drew in the sand. He made a line for the trail to sacred Blue Lake. He showed how the trail went up and up and up through the mountains. Father said, "Some day when you are older, you will go there with the men of your village. You will go there to learn things that only an Indian may know."

Tso'u listened to all that his father told him. He felt happy and strong and good. He felt "growing-up." After a little while of thinking he whispered low to his father, "I think that lake is calling me to come. I want to go there."

Now it was his father's turn for thinking. All was quiet and still while father sat, and thought, with his small boy between his knees. At last he answered Tso'u. He said, "I can see no reason why you and Pachole can not make that journey. The trail is long, but you are strong." Then Father thought some more. He told his little boy to go out in the plaza and play with the other boys. He told him, "Tomorrow will be an important day." But that was all that he would say, just, "Wait for tomorrow."

Tso'u went to the plaza to play a little, and to wait for the slow coming of to-morrow. Sun Old Man moved on lazy feet. But at last he put himself away behind the mountains.

Night came . . . and sleep. Then it was morning. It was yesterday's tomorrow.

Ann Nolan Clark

Rain Pond
**Danielle Martinez,
age 9, Tewa**

SPIRIT WORLD OF THE ZUNIS

Many years ago, when I was still a young lad, I was taken to the place of our ancestors' dwellings. About twenty-six miles west of Zuni there stands a lone hill amidst the quiet solitude of rolling plains. It took us a day and a half to reach the hill where the spirits of our Zuni people go to rest after their deaths. When we reached our destination, a door led into the hill. This door has been seen only when the cults of the six kivas go there to offer the spirits blessings and in turn ask for the livelihood of the Zuni people. When these people came near the hill, there appeared to be a door leading into four rooms that are designated as the way the Zuni people emerged onto the surface of the earth.

When we entered, we found the first room with floors of clean limestone. The doors were narrow and small. There in the first room we planted prayersticks and came back out. The priests stood side by side along the places where they had planted their prayersticks. They told us, "Come, we will take you up on this hill to show you what lies on the other side."

We went up on the hill and looked over to see fields of corn, melon, and a great abundance of other crops. Then we came down the hill where the spirits of the Mudheads dwell. When we came farther down, we came to a spring where water ran free, down to the fields. After we saw the fields and came back to the spring, the two priests of the kivas, of which one was my brother, had to go into the spring. They undressed and took their sacred corn pouches and proceeded into the spring. When they neared the opening from which the spring came, they exclaimed that there had been someone who entered not long before them. The tracks proved to be those of a female.

The two men went on in murmuring prayers while they went on farther. As the priests went in, there came a flock of white geese coming down, joining with us. When the priests had finished their rituals in the spring and the rest of us completed what we were supposed to do, the priests came out and we started back home. But the flock of geese we saw has never again approached the spring. For the year we had gone to ask for blessings, we received rains, crops flourished, and there were no hardships. Only once had the flock of geese been seen and they were spoken of as a good omen.

OPPOSITE:
Untitled (Taos)
Ellison Hoover

Not long after, however, the priests became angry with each other, starting disputes that divided the Zuni people. There came many conflicts, and hardships grew to a point where the whole Zuni populace suffered.

Because of seeing the good omen, which was believed to be the source of prosperity, the Zunis every four years go to the Koh-thlou-wah-la-wah to give offering for the blessings of fertility of the land and peace among the Zuni people.

The Zuni people, translated by Alvina Quam

Zuni Planting
W. J. Metcalf

PRAYER TO THE ANCIENTS AFTER HARVESTING

From where you stay quietly,
Your little wind–blown clouds,
Your fine wisps of clouds,
Your massed clouds you will send forth
    to sit down with us;
With your fine rain caressing the earth,
With all your waters
You will pass to us on our roads.
With your great pile of waters,
With your fine rain caressing the earth,
You will pass to us on our roads.
My fathers,
Add to your hearts.
Your waters,
Your seeds,
Your long life,
Your old age
You will grant to us.
Therefore I have added to your hearts,
To the end, my fathers,
My children:
You will protect us.
All my ladder–descending children
Will finish their roads;
They will grow old.
You will bless us with life.

Zuni poem, translated by Margot Astrov

THE PINE GUM BABY

There is a telling that one spring Coyote decided to grow some melons. He planted the seeds and tended the young vines, and whenever he was not out hunting, he was working in his melon patch.

One morning, when the fat melons were almost ready to gather, he found that two of them had been stolen. Coyote growled and looked all around the patch but could find not a single track because the vines were so thick they covered the ground.

Next morning, two more melons were gone. This time, Coyote searched harder than before, and at last he found some scratches where someone had squeezed under the fence.

"Ah, here is where the thief came in," he cried. "I'll fix him, that Rabbit Boy."

So he trotted off to a large pinyon tree and gathered a jar full of pine gum. He shaped the gum into a baby and set it near the hole under the fence.

That night, Rabbit came quietly in the moonlight as he had before. But when he crawled through the hole and saw the gum baby sitting in his way, he was a little annoyed.

"Good evening," he said, pretending politeness. "Will you be so kind as to let me pass?"

But the gum baby neither answered his greeting nor moved aside.

"Good evening, I say, will you let me pass?"

Still gum baby did not move. Rabbit was more annoyed than ever. He lifted his paw and gave the gum baby a shove, but his paw stuck fast.

"Turn me loose," shouted Rabbit as he pulled and tugged to get away. "Turn me loose, or I'll hit you again."

But the gum baby held him fast. So Rabbit hit him as hard as he could with the other paw. It stuck as fast as the first.

"Maybe you think I can't kick you," he cried. "You had better turn me loose before I kick you." And Rabbit hauled off and kicked as hard as he could. There was his foot, stuck fast. This made him so angry that he kicked fiercely with his other foot, and then it was stuck, too.

"I will butt you," raged Rabbit, butting the gum baby with his head. And it stuck, too. So there he was, stuck fast to that gum baby. He rolled and struggled to get loose but only stuck faster than ever.

When the sun came up, Coyote ran out to see if he had caught Rabbit. "So, I have caught you at last Rabbit Boy. Now I shall eat you for stealing my melons."

"I was only passing by," said Rabbit. "And this gum baby was so rude I had to hit him. Please take me off."

"I will eat you off," said Coyote.

"Well, I would not taste very good," said Rabbit. "I am all sticky."

"I guess that's right," said Coyote. "I'll have to take you down by the river and wash you off."

And so he did.

"Now I shall have a good meal," said Coyote.

"But please don't eat me here," begged Rabbit. "The rains would carry my bones away and scatter them so that I could never come to life again. Then you would have no more rabbit to eat."

"Where can I eat you, then?" asked Coyote.

"Put me down for a minute so I can think," said Rabbit.

When Coyote put him down, Rabbit bounded away beyond Coyote's reach.

That is how it happened that the trick was turned upon himself.

WORSHIPPING WATER

They (the Zuni) perform rites and sacrifices to certain idols, but what they most worship is water, to which they offer painted sticks and plumes, or bunches of yellow flowers; and this they do commonly at springs. They also offer turquoises, which are, however, poor in quality.

Pedro de Casteñeda

**Santa Clara tale,
retold by Evelyn Dahl Reed**
from *Coyote Tales from the Indian Pueblos*, Sunstone Press

IRRIGATION

When my Father
needs water
For his thirsty fields,
He opens the ditches
To let the water run slowly,
Slowly,
Around the roots
Of all the growing things.

My Father
Closes the ditches
To stop the water,
When his fields
Have finished drinking.

My Father
Opens the ditches
When it is his day
To irrigate his fields.

No one
Would take a day
That was not his
To irrigate.

No one
Would take too much water
When it was his day
To irrigate.

All Indians
Are taught,
When they are little,
That water is good;
It must not be wasted.

I have known this
For a long time.

Ann Nolan Clark

OPPOSITE:
*Oyegi-a'Ye (Frost
Moving), Governor,
Santa Clara (1905)*
Edward S. Curtis

RATTLESNAKE FOOLS WITH COYOTE

Coyote was out hunting and met Rattlesnake. They were going along when Coyote said, "Come over to my house tomorrow. We will eat together."

The next morning, Rattlesnake came over. He moved slowly around the floor of Coyote's lodge and shook his tail. Coyote sat over to one side when he heard this. He did not like it. It made him afraid. Finally Rattlesnake settled down.

Coyote put a big kettle of hot rabbit stew down in front of Rattlesnake. "Here, eat, my friend. You'll like this."

"No, I cannot eat this. I do not understand your food."

"What food do you eat?"

"I eat the yellow flowers of the corn."

Coyote was surprised at this but he looked around for some yellow pollen. When he found some, Rattlesnake said, "That's good. Now put some on my nose so that I can eat it." Coyote stood off as far as possible from the snake and put a little on the top of Rattlesnake's nose. "Come over here," said Rattlesnake, "and put enough on my nose so that I can find it." He rattled a little, and Coyote jumped back afraid, but after a while he came closer and put some more pollen on Rattlesnake's nose.

When he'd finished eating, Rattlesnake said, "I am going now. Tomorrow you come over to my house and eat."

Coyote thought about what Rattlesnake had done and how afraid he had been to get near Rattlesnake. The next day, before leaving for Rattlesnake's house, he put some pebbles in a gourd and tied the gourd to his tail. Then he went on his way, moving on his belly like a snake. This is how he came into Rattlesnake's house, with his hand shaking his tail to make the sound of the rattle.

When Coyote shook his rattle, the snake said, "Oh, my friend, I am afraid when you do that." Rattlesnake had a stew of mice on the fire and he put these in front of Coyote, being careful to stay back as far as possible, as though he were afraid to get too close to Coyote. Coyote showed his teeth. Rattlesnake jumped back fast. Then he said, "Please, my companion, eat some of my food."

"I cannot eat your food because I do not understand it."

Rattlesnake insisted, but Coyote refused the food. He said, "If you will put some of the flower of the corn on my head I will eat it. That's the kind of food I eat. I understand that."

Rattlesnake got some corn pollen but he pretended to be afraid of getting too close to Coyote.

"Come nearer, my friend. Put that corn pollen on my head."

"I am afraid of you."

"Come nearer, I am not bad."

Rattlesnake came up to Coyote and put the pollen on top of his nose. Coyote tried to get it with his tongue. But he did not have a tongue like the snake's and he could not reach the pollen. He tried many times, putting his tongue up on one side of his nose and then the other, but he couldn't reach the pollen. The snake had turned away to conceal his laughing. Finally, Coyote said he was not really hungry and would eat later. He began to leave and took hold of his tail and shook his rattle. The snake backed off and said, "Oh, my companion, I am so afraid."

Later Coyote was still crawling along on his belly like a snake. "I was such a fool. The snake had a good stew, lots of it, and I wouldn't eat any. Now I am just hungry."

He went on like that, trying to find something to eat.

Barry Lopez

Tanning the hide
Alfonso Roybal
(a.k.a. Awa Tsireh)

ON THE ROOF THROWING

The family members take boxes of the throw goods to the roof. There are many boxes heaped with crackers, cookies, candy, soda pop, melons, balloons, beach balls, canned food, and many other items. What is being thrown today is quite different from what was thrown a century ago.

And as it is a summer throw, buckets and hoses are also carried to the roof, and the buckets are filled with water.

Soon the village people gather around the house and the throwing begins. The very young children in the family cannot really throw, but they are given pieces of candy and soft items to drop over the sides of the roof. The adults on the roof throw in all directions to the calls from below of, "Over here! Throw over here!" And when a bucket of water is thrown over the roof everyone below shrieks and laughs and jumps aside.

No one below knows what will come over the roof next—something good to eat or water to soak the clothes and drench the hair.

Cochiti tale, retold by Kris Hotvedt
from *Pueblo and Navajo Indian Life Today*, Sunstone Press

THE HARVESTING OF CORN IS BEGUN

Once upon a time when the world was young, all the inhabitants had the same tasks. They made their living by fishing, hunting, and agricultural pursuits. They harvested much food, but as yet they did not know the use of corn.

Thus, when the star gods wanted to give the People knowledge of the use of corn, they assembled to decide which group should receive the knowledge of this food. After thinking it over in silence, Moyachuntanah, the Great Star, said, "Let all the People come together and participate in a race. Let each group choose its best runner, and whoever wins the race, his group shall be given the use of corn." This seemed like a good plan to the star gods, and they agreed to follow it.

All the people from the nearby pueblos were called together and their runners

Cleaning the ditch
**Joe Evan Duran
(Po–re Pien), Tesuque**

chosen, one from Zuni, another from Acoma, and also a Navajo. Moyachuntanah picked an ear of corn and broke it in three parts. Of the three, the tip of the ear was the shortest, the center part somewhat longer, and the end the longest.

Finally, when the runners were ready, the three pieces were placed hear the three runners. The signal was given for the start of the race. The three started out as swiftly as deer. The people surrounding them gazed at them with admiration, each group anxious for its chosen runner to win.

From the start, the Navajo ran swiftly and was the first to reach the ear of corn cut in three parts. He chose the tip, the runner from Zuni the center piece, and the runner from Acoma the end.

The older brother of the Great Star, Mokwanosenah, the Morning Star, nodded his head approvingly on seeing that the Navajo was the victor. "Clearly," he said, "the Navajo has won the race." But Moyachuntanah, the Great Star, spoke thus: "Although the Navajo won the race, he selected the smallest piece of corn; he cannot be given the prize. The Navajos will always roam from place to place and will never have the time for sowing and harvesting. The Zunis and Acomas always attend their fields and, consequently, it is better to give them the use of the corn."

And thus it has been since remote times, exactly as stated by the Great Star. The Navajos are always on the road and do not occupy themselves in harvesting. They make their living at other occupations. They have their winter homes and their summer homes in different locations. As to the Zunis and the Acomas, they reside in their respective pueblos and always live by sowing and harvesting. Corn has always been one of their most important items of food.

Carmen Gertrudis Espinosa

PART FOUR

ABODE
OF SOULS

REMINISCING WITH PÁ-PA (GRANDMOTHER) ABOUT KA-TSE-MA

"Try to remember, *Pá-pa*, as I will also try to remember, when the old ones of *Aco-matra* (people of Acoma) were very well off spiritually and in harmony with everything around them."

So *Pá-pa* reminds me of the peaceful times, when *Acomatra* lived on *Ka-tse-ma*. "The mountains around *Acó* were also in harmony with all that was around them—the four–leggeds, the trees and the rocks. Our fields were plentiful with crops. Our people were strong at this peaceful time."

Pueblo House (1920)
Velino Shije Herrera

Pá-pa reminds me of the time before our people had ever seen *Ma-tash-cana*. I give *Pá-pa* my undivided attention, amazed at the seriousness in her beautiful squinting black eyes. "If your *Na-Na* (Grandfather) were alive, he would have told you this story, for it teaches many things.

"It is good to know this story of the old ones. They have taught us to try and correct our mistakes at times when we are most fortunate. Greed is one thing the old ones told us to be careful of. We, as *Acomatra*, should never have that greed enter our lives.

"There was a most sorrowful incident that happened at this time when our people were most happy. It has been said greed made us lose two generations of our loved ones on *Ka-tse-ma*."

"At this time it was decided that the *Pá-pas* would stay on *Ka-tse-ma* with the babies while the healthy ones were working in the fields on the valley floor. You see, as I am getting old in my years, I am unable to do the work in the fields as I used to when I was young. The *Pá-pas* were like me, unable to work in the fields. The babies were too young.

"The young healthy ones who were busily working in the fields below *Ka-tse-ma* overworked the land. The rains had been good that spring and had provided good moisture for a good growing season. The old ones said we had enough crops to feed everyone on *Ka-tse-ma* for the coming winter. However, our people continued to overwork Mother Earth."

"One day, while our young ones worked in the fields, a rainstorm approached Acoma Valley. But the young ones ignored the approaching storm and continued working.

"Soon rain was pouring from the sky like *Acomatra* had never seen before. The fields began to erode. As our people ran back to the stairway which went to the top of *Ka-tse-ma*, they found it was washed out by the tremendous rain. Thunder roared in the sky. Jagged formations of lightning lit up the sky.

"The concern turned to the old ones and young ones on top of *Ka-tse-ma*. Everyone panicked and began to weep, and as the people wept, the storm be–came worse, destroying our crops, and the stairway was completely washing out. The rain continued for many days, causing great sorrow among our people. Some became very sick and died.

"You see, *Pá-pa*, our people felt the sorrow after it was too late. The greed shown by our people in overworking Mother Earth caused a separating of our people. By making the judgment that some of us were too weak to help out is something Great Spirit had to teach us out of that experience.

"We lost two generations, and it caused great sorrow, but Great Spirit had a reason for this. Without our old ones, we are weak, just like the young ones who were left with the old ones. And without our young, we lost strength in a generation we had already created to carry on the teachings the old ones would have handed down to them.

"This is why we tell you today to respect your elders, respect the unborn, respect the young, respect Mother Earth and all that is around her. At that time, when our bellies were full, we wanted still more. So you see, grandson, Great Spirit watches over us, but when we abuse Mother Earth by overworking her, it is wrong.

"The old ones learned many ways of respect after this sorrowful time of our people. This is why I tell you this today. The hardest part of our people to overcome was to hear our ancestors crying on top of *Ka-tse-ma*. There was nothing they could do but cry too and ask Great Spirit to help us overcome our ignorance.

FAMOUS LOST WORDS

There are many traditions connected with this old church, one of which is that it was built by a race of giants, fifty feet in height. But these, dying off, they were succeeded by dwarfs, with red heads who, being in their turn exterminated, were followed by the Aztecs.

Pvt. Josiah M. Rice
(on Pecos Pueblo Church, 1851)

"This is why we listened very intently to one of the four birds of wisdom who told us to move to *Acó*, where we now sit—and we should give our thanksgiving every day to Great Spirit for allowing us to become a strong people after this sorrowful incident. We also give thanks to the ones who were left on *Ka-tse-ma* so that we could correct our mistake of greed.

"If you listen sometimes, *Pá-pa*, you will hear these old ones on *Ka-tse-ma* calling us and advising us. Listen to them, *Pá-pa*, for you will learn from them. Their advice is said to always be good, for they were the last of our people to live on our most beloved *Ka-tse-ma*.

"You will be a man soon, *Pá-pa*, remember all these things. They are for your own good. In your lifetime you will encounter these situations. I always look back at this story of the great suffering of our people. I am old, but this story makes me grateful for my lifetime. I hope it will make you grateful for yours. And always remember to respect all that is around you, for this is the greatest lesson *Acomatra* were taught by Great Spirit. Remember our lost generations."

Manuel Pino
Acoma

Rainbow Pueblo
Eliza Morse, age 11, Tewa

A WOMAN MOURNS FOR HER HUSBAND

They came. They brought the ones who had been killed by the white people. My aunts were with me. My mother, my father, my aunts, held me and went with me. I came there; I was pregnant. They would not let me see him, my husband. Only my mother saw him. She told me. It was not good. . . . So they buried them in the graveyard, just before sunset.

My grandfather took care of me. "It is very dangerous; you must fast. You must drink medicine. You must vomit. It is very dangerous. No one may touch you. It is very dangerous, you must fast. No one must touch you. You must stay alone. You must sit alone in the corner. Only your little boy may hold you. No one must touch you." Grandfather gathered medicine for me. This he soaked. He mixed it in a fine bowl. He brewed medicine. "This you will drink. You will vomit," he said to me. I was very wretched. This was very dangerous. When it was still early, when the sun had not yet risen, my grandfather took me far away. We scattered prayermeal. Here in the left hand I had black prayermeal, and here the right kind of prayermeal. When we had gone far I passed it four times over my head and scattered it. One should not speak. Again with this, I sprinkled prayer-meal with a prayer:

My fathers,
Our sun Father.
Our mother, Dawn,
Coming out standing to your sacred place,
Somewhere we shall pass you on your road.
This from which we form our flesh,
The white corn,
Prayermeal,
Shell,
Corn pollen,
I offer to you.
To the Sun who is our father,
To you I offer it

To you, I offer prayermeal.

To you, I offer corn pollen.

According to the words of my prayer,

So may it be.

May there be no deviation.

Sincerely from my heart I send forth my prayers.

To you, prayermeal, shell, I offer.

Corn pollen I offer.

According to the words of my prayer,

So may it be.

I would sprinkle prayermeal. I would inhale from the prayermeal. I would sprinkle the right kind of prayermeal. . . .

Alone I sat. I did not eat meat, nor salt, nor grease. I fasted from the meat. It was very dangerous. Much my aunt, my grandfather exhorted me. When I was young, they said to me, "Fortunate you are to be alive. Sometimes you will be happy because of something. Sometimes you will be sorrowful. You will cry. This kind of person you shall be. You are fortunate to be alive." And just so I have lived . . . If one's husband dies one will not sleep. She will lie down as if she sleeps, and when the sleep overcomes her she will sleep. But after a little while she will wake, and will not sleep. She will cry, she will be lonely. She will not care to eat. She will take thought of what to do and where to go. When a child or relative dies, one cries for them properly. Husband and wife talk together to relieve their thoughts. Then they will forget their trouble. But when one's husband dies there is no happiness. . . .

It was very dangerous. It was the same as when an enemy dies, it was very dangerous. Four mornings I vomited. And so many days I sprinkled prayermeal far off, four times. And so many days I fasted. I was still a young woman. . . .

For one year I would cry. I was thoughtful for my old husband. Then father spoke with me. I was happy. I did not worry. My uncle desired it for me. "It is all right, niece. Do not cry. It cannot be helped. It is ever thus. Do not think of where you have come from, but rather look forward to where you are to go. . . ."

Zuni tale, retold by Margot Astrov

Sia War Dancer
(1925)
Edward S. Curtis

GRANDMOTHER

Grandmother
before i learned to crawl
you turned golden
like an aspen leaf
and flew away
from my open arms . . .

Joseph L. Concha, Taos
from *Chokecherry Hunters and Other Poems*, Sunstone Press

Iahla (Willow), Taos (1905)
Edward S. Curtis

OLD WOMAN

Old Woman,
It is you.
It was you even when
I did not see you except
In the eyes of my spirit.
Old Woman,
With you I saw
The dead log giving life
And the mid-winter stream
Rippling up for spring and
The mountains a long way off
Telling us of beginnings.
Old Woman,
With you I knew
The peace of high places
And the meaning of a flower
Curled up against the wind
Or leaning toward the sun.

Old Woman,
In small things always
There was you as if
All nature contained your thoughts and so
I learned from rocks and rainbows,
Tall trees and butterflies.
Old Woman,
There was you in the eagle
Flying free and lonely,
And in the eyes of a deer
I saw once in an untamed place.
Old Woman,
There is you in all good things
That awaken me and say
My life was richer, fuller
Because you lived with me.

Nancy Wood

THE OLD WOMAN

For in those days there was one A'shiwi who could not, because of years of misfortunes, share in the plenty of the people. She was an old mother who lived down at the bottom of the village in a fallen–down house. Her brothers had all been killed in wars and her husband was dead of a disease, and she didn't have any daughters to bring their husbands into her home, and all her sons had moved away to live with the families of their wives, and all had forgotten her. So she lived alone, with no one to help her plant her corn seeds, or to water the plants, and she was very poor. The old woman had no men to bring her deer hides, and no way to get cotton. So her clothing was rags. The people of the village threw their trash and garbage down the slope to get rid of it, and it fell all around her house, and even on her roof. So she had to spend much of her time every morning cleaning it up.

That's what she was doing when she saw the Corn Maidens coming out of the village. At first she didn't say anything to them, because the people of the village didn't like her to talk to them or to be around where they could see her. The A'shiwi were rich, now, and the ragged old mother reminded them how it had been when they were poor. But quickly, the old woman saw that the Corn Maidens looked cold and ragged and old and tired, and hungry, too. She thought they wouldn't mind. So she shouted to them in her old, weak voice.

"Come in and sit happy," she said. "Your hunger will put good taste in the poor food I can offer you tonight. Come in and sit happy by my fire, and be satisfied with my little food and rest yourself. And tomorrow it will be better for you. For tomorrow the people of Ha'wi–k'uh will hold a great feast and a great game at which all the good food will be thrown around as if it were nothing but mud from the river. Tomorrow you can go back into the village and pick up all you wish to eat from the ground. But tonight, your great hunger will add taste to my poor food."

So the Corn Maidens came in and the old woman took off her ragged blanket and spread it on the floor for them to sit upon. She put the cornmeal she had boiled for her own supper into a bowl for them and worked straightening out things around the room—the way women do—so her guests wouldn't notice there was nothing for her to eat. But the Yellow Corn Maiden noticed anyway.

"An old mother as kind and gentle as you should not go without your supper," the Yellow Corn Maiden said. "Sit happy here and join us at this meal because we, too, have some food."

Then the White Corn Maiden brought from under her torn blanket a pouch made of buckskin and beaded with turquoise and the whitest shells. From that, she took out honeycomb, corn cakes, and the bread that is made with meal and piñon nuts. Then she took out a pouch of pollen and sprinkled it over the old woman's lumpy cornmeal mush. A mist rose up from the pot and it smelled like a meadow of spring flowers. And when the old mother saw this happen, she knew that these poor women must be two of the Corn Maidens, or two of the other Beloved Ones whom A'wonawil'ona made to help look after the A'shiwi. The old mother felt ashamed that she had been so bold as to invite the Beloved Ones into her broken old house. She huddled over by the wall away from them.

Then the Yellow Corn Maiden spoke to her. "Old mother, know now who we

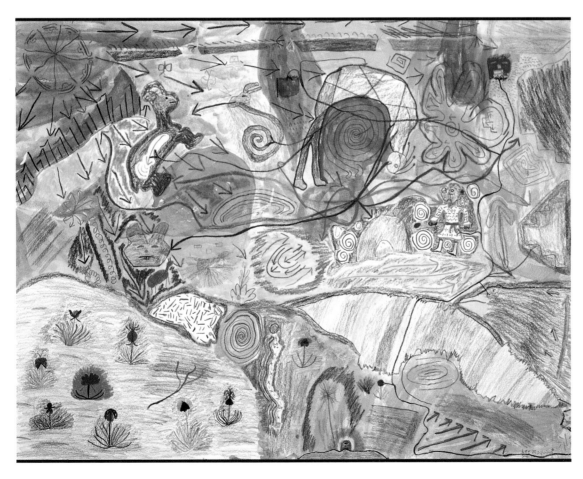

Ancient Ancestors
**Lee Moquino, age 10,
Tewa**

are and know why we come here. We are Yellow Corn Maiden and White Corn Maiden, and we come to look at our children, the A'shiwi, the Flesh of the Flesh. But now we find that you and two little ones up in the village must be the only true A'shiwi who are left in Ha'wi–k'uh. So come, sit happy with us and be satisfied. You asked us to eat with you. We ask you now to eat with us."

The old mother was still afraid, but she got out her prayer meal and sprinkled it on the heads of the Corn Maidens, blessing them. And as she sat to eat with them, she saw their hair was no longer grizzled with the age, but black and glossy with youth, and their wrists jangled with perfect silver, and their faces were beautiful with happiness. The old mother dipped her fingers into the coarse corn mush and found it had become sweet and rich to taste, as if it had been mixed with honey. And the Corn Maidens talked to her and laughed and made jokes. The old mother's lonely old heart forgot its years of solitude and remembered how it had been when her sons had been around her and her house had been full of the sounds of children.

When they had all satisfied themselves, the White Corn Maiden brought out a bundle and unrolled it on the floor. Inside was a white cape of fringed doeskin. "Hang this on your blanket pole, kind mother," the White Corn Maiden said, "and on the morning after you hang it there, you will find under it meal, and melons, and all good things to eat, in plenty. We leave you this because our water blessing will no longer come to Ha'wi–k'uh." By then Sun Father had left the sky and gone to his sacred place, and darkness covered Corn Mountain, and the Corn Maidens breathed on the hands of the old mother, and she breathed on their hands, and they went away.

Zuni tale, retold by Tony Hillerman

OPPOSITE:
Santana Quitana, Cochiti
(1925)
Edward S. Curtis

SACRED SHOES

When I was very small, my great-grandmother told me a version of this story about a very advanced medicine woman. (Or was she really a supernatural? But if she was, how could the story end that way?) I remembered pieces of it, especially the part about how she shakes out her moccasins, maybe because Grandma Gunn's gestures were graphic at that point. I can see her still, pointing to her shoe and shaking her hand as though holding it.

Long ago, the people suffered from a terrible sickness. It was a sickness that made them break out all over with sores, and many died.

They had heard about a great healer woman who lived to the southwest of them. Her name was Qiyo Kepe, and she lived far to the south of them in a house that had leaves for a roof. The people sent a runner to bring her to their village so she could cure Yellow Woman. The runner was dispatched, and after some time he found her home and persuaded her to return to the village with him.

At the edge of the first river they came to, one that flowed swift and deep, Qiyo Kepe took off one of her moccasins to shake the sand out of it, and herds of deer, antelope, buffalo, and all the other animals of the forests and plains sprang into life. This frightened the messenger, and he hurried the old woman along. They rushed across the river and traveled as fast as he could urge her until they came to another river. Again she removed her moccasin and shook it, and birds flew forth from the wind her shaking made, singing. The messenger became even more frightened.

Again, when they came to a third river, she took off her moccasins, and as she shook it reptiles of all kinds came forth, springing into life from the specks of sand that she shook from her shoe. At this sight the messenger was even more terrified, and more than that, he was enraged.

At the fourth river, Qiyo Kepe again shook out her moccasin, and this time insects of every kind buzzed forth. In a mindless panic, the messenger hurried with the terrifying woman to the village where Yellow Woman was waiting for death.

Qiyo Kepe set to work immediately, bathing the sores on Yellow Woman's body with pure water from the nearby spring. That was all she used, but she used a lot of it, continuously bathing the young woman, and in four days Yellow

Woman was well. Qiyo Kepe then turned her attention to the others. She told the women what to do, and because of her knowledge, all who were alive when she arrived in the village were healed.

Meantime the village men had been talking. They were angry that this woman could heal with water when all their medicine and incantations had failed. The medicine men's society was especially angry. So they told the messenger to take her home, then to pretend he had returned to the village. But he was to go to the river nearest her home and bring back a party of men who would be waiting there. They would return to the old woman's house and kill her, because they believed that only in this way could their power and the people's confidence in them be restored.

So they did as planned, but when the party returned to Qiyo Kepe's house, she met them at the door and asked them to come in. They refused, but said they would come back in four days to kill her and all of her family.

Hearing this, Qiyo Kepe took up the broom that was leaning against the door-jamb and began to sweep. As she swept, she sang a chant that went "Qiyo Kepe is not like you. Qiyo Kepe is one who knows. Generations will come and generations will go, before your disease's scars no longer show, before you will return to faith, because you have murdered Qiyo Kepe."

When the fourth day had passed, the men returned to Qiyo Kepe's home. They murdered the old woman and her brother and all of their families.

And when Qiyo Kepe was dead, all the animals began to mourn: the birds dropped their wings and were silent, the herds slunk away into the brush and the forests and remained unseen, the bees and the other insects rasped their mourning, and all the reptiles crawled away and hid themselves.

Paula Gunn Allen
Laguna/Sioux

NOW GOD HAS DIED

All the Indians of the pueblos of the Pecos [have rebelled and are] saying that now God and Holy Mary, whom the Spaniards worshipped, had died, but the god they obeyed had never died, and therefore they would take possession of the kingdom, having done with all the Spaniards.

Santa Fe Municipal Council, 1697

THE ABODE OF SOULS

Not long did the impetuous Bear and Crane clan fathers deliberate, but straight-away strode into the red waters feeling with their feet for footing as they led the way across. Yet their fearfulness was great for as they watched, the waters moved beneath them, strange chills and feelings beset them as though they were beginning to change into the forms of hidden water creatures. Nevertheless they won their way to the opposite shore. The poor women with children on their backs were more susceptible to the aura of these strange waters and became panic-stricken and witless with fear. The children, being as yet unfinished and imma-ture, changed instantly in their terror. Their skins turned cold and scaly and they grew tails. Their hands and feet became webbed and clawed as if for swimming in those disquieting waters. To their mothers the children felt like dead things that scratched and clung on their bare shoulders. Shrieking wildly, the mothers cast their children away and fled in terror.

Wailing piteously, many of the children fell into the swift waters. Their shrill and plaintive calls could be heard even from under the water—as it is said they may still be heard at night near lonely waters.

No sooner did they sink beneath the waters than they changed even more. Some became lizards, others frogs, turtles or newts. But their souls, their inner beings, sank through the waters of the lagoon below the hollow mountain of the Koyemshi into the abode of ghosts, Hápanawan, where the finished souls of an-cient men of war and violent death resided. There also was the pueblo of Kóth-luwalawan, the town of towns, with its great six-chambered assembly house of the spirits, wherein the god priests sat in council. It was there also that the priests taught to the newly dead the Kókokshi, or Dance of Good, and from them also received the messages and offerings of mortal men.

Now when the little ones sank into the dark depths, the lights of the spirit dancers began to break upon them and they became as the ancients. Having been received by these undying ones, they thus made the pathway that all the dead must follow. But the mothers, not knowing their children had returned un-harmed to the spirit world where in time they too would go, loudly wailed on the far shore of the river.

The Seed clans were the next to arrive and they also strove to cross the waters only to meet the same dismal fate. Upon witnessing this, the Macaw and the other midmost clans fled southward looking for a better crossing and were soon lost from view, never to be seen again.

As the people wailed and mourned their lost children, the Beloved Twins returned and with strong sounding voices bade them cease their clamor and terror. They advised all mothers to cherish their children through all dangers and not behave like birds, abandoning their offspring at the first threat. "For," they said, "the magic of the waters will pass through the river." The mothers took heart and, clutching their children to them, they won their way through the waters to the opposite shore.

Now when the people were rested and the remaining children calmed, they arose and journeyed into the plain east of the mountains with the great water between. Thence they turned northward to camp on the sunrise slopes of the uppermost mountains. Mourning their lost children, they also awaited the ones who had fled southward, but those never returned.

**Zuni tale, retold by
Frank Hamilton Cushing**

*Wahu Toya, Pecos,
at Jemez* (1880)
John K. Hillers

HOW THE DAYS WILL BE

Indeed, the enemy,
Though in his life
He was a person given to falsehood,
He has become one to foretell
How the world will be,
How the days will be.
That during his time
We may have good days,
Beautiful days
Hoping for this,
We shall keep his days.
Indeed, if we are lucky,
During the enemy's time
Fine rain caressing the earth,
Heavy rain caressing the earth,
We shall win.
When the enemy's days are in progress,
The enemy's waters

We shall win,
His seeds we shall win,
His riches we shall win,
His power,
His strong spirit,
His long life,
His old age,
In order to win these,
Tirelessly, unwearied,
We shall pass his days.
Now, indeed, the enemy,
Even one who thought himself a man,
In a shower of arrows,
In a shower of war clubs,
With bloody hear,
The enemy,
Reaching the end of his life,
Added to the flesh of our earth mother.

Zuni poem, collected by John Bierhorst

THE BORROWED FEATHERS

One day the Bluebirds were busy grinding corn. Coyote came along and said he wanted to grind corn too. The birds knew he didn't know how to do this, but they let him do it anyway.

In the middle of the day it got very hot. "Let's all go up on top of that mesa over there and get a cool drink of water," said the birds. "What shall we do with our friends here?" asked one of the birds. "He has no feathers. He can't fly up there. We must give him some of our feathers." So they gave him feathers and showed him how to fly.

Then they all flew off to the mesa.

"Let's get there before Coyote does," said one of the birds. "He always has some dirty stuff around his mouth. He will make the water bad." They got there before Coyote and had a drink and then Coyote flew in. "Let's take back the feathers," said one of the Bluebirds, "and leave Coyote up here." Everyone thought that would be pretty good. They took their feathers back and left.

Coyote wandered around all day trying to find a way off the mesa. Finally he tried to jump down in one place but it was too steep. He fell to the bottom and killed himself. Later the Bluebirds wondered if Coyote ever got off the mesa and they flew over to see. When they saw he was dead they were afraid he might try to use bad medicine against them, so they made him come back to life again.

They do this every time Coyote is killed.

Barry Lopez

Two birds
Louis Gonzales

THE ORIGIN OF DEATH

They were coming up from Shipap. One of their children became sick and they did not know what was the trouble with him. They had never seen sickness before. They said to the Shkoyo (curing society) chief, "Perhaps our Mother in Shipap will help us. Go back and ask her to take away this trouble." He went back to our Mother and she said to him, "The child is dead. If your people did not die, the world would fill up and there would be no place for you to live. When you die, you will come back to Shipap to live with me. Keep on traveling and do not be troubled when your people die."

He returned to his people and told them what our Mother had said. In those days they treated one another as brothers, all the Indians of all the Pueblos. They planted corn with the digging stick and they were never tired; they dug trenches to irrigate their fields. The corn ripened in one day. When they came to Frijoles they separated, and the different pueblos went their own ways.

Buck and three coyotes
Ascensión H. Galvan

Cochiti tale, collected by Margot Astrov

SONG OF A CHILD'S SPIRIT

I am on the way,

traveling the road to where the spirits live,

at Shipap.

I look at the road, far ahead, down that way.

Nothing happens to me, as I am a spirit.

I am a spirit, of course I am,

as I go on the nice clean road to Shipap.

It is true that my spirit meets the others

who come towards me.

I am glad to see them and be with them,

I have a right to be there.

I cannot help it; I must leave because the

   spirit

has called me back.

I must go, I must obey.

I am going direct to my spirit.

There are places down there where all the people

live whom you have seen;

they have gone, when the time has come.

Now I cannot say what they will make of me.

I may take the form of a cloud;

I wish I could be a cloud.

I take the chance of whatever is offered to me.

When a cloud comes this way, you will say,

"That is he!"

When I get to the place of spirits,

I will hear everything you ask.

You must always remember me.

You have talked about me,

and in Shipap I can hear everything you

   say.

I am a spirit and I bless you.

I thank you for all you have done for me in

   past years.

I hope to see you some day.

We send you many good wishes, many good

   things.

Thank you.

**Santo Domingo poem,
collected by Margot Astrov**

A VERY GOOD DAY TO DIE

Today is a very good day to die.
Every living thing is in harmony with me.
Every voice sings a chorus within me.
All beauty has come to rest in my eyes.
All bad thoughts have departed from me.
Today is a very good day to die.
My land is peaceful around me.
My fields have been turned for the last time.
My house is filled with laughter.
My children have come home.
Yes, today is a very good day to die.

Nancy Wood

PART FIVE

PUEBLO

CONQUISTADOR HOSPITALITY, 1540

Editor's Note: In the summer of 1540, Coronado, leading an army of conquistadors and Catholic friars, arrived at Tiguex along the Rio Grande, the site of present day Bernalillo, in search of the fabled Seven Cities of Gold. For six months the Spaniards waged all-out war against the peaceful natives and pillaged their twelve simple mud villages, leaving them starving, diseased, and destitute. The following account, written by Pedro de Casteñeda, the expedition chronicler, is the earliest known record of Spanish brutality against the Pueblo Indians of New Mexico.

Give us your clothing

The general wished to obtain some clothing to divide among his soldiers, and for this purpose he summoned one of the chief Indians of Tiguex. . . . The general told him he must furnish about three hundred or more pieces of cloth, which he needed to give his people. He (the chief) said he was not able to do this . . . that they would have to consult together and divide it among the villages, and that it was necessary to make the demand among each town separately. . . . As they were in very great need, they did not give the natives a chance to consult about it, but when they came to a village they demanded what they had to give, so that they could proceed at once. Thus these people could do nothing except take off their own cloaks and give them to make the number that they demanded of them. And some of the soldiers . . . if they saw any Indian with a better one on, they exchanged with him without any more ado, not stopping to find out the rank of the man they were stripping, which caused not a little hard feeling.

Give us your women

Besides what I have just said, one whom I will not name, out of regard for him, left the village where the camp was and went to another village about a league distant, and seeing a pretty woman there he called her husband down to hold his horse by the bridle while he went up. . . . While he was there, the Indian heard some slight noise, and then the Spaniard came down, took his horse, and went away. The Indian went up and learned that the Spaniard had violated, or tried to violate, his wife, and so he came with the important men of the town to com–plain that a man had violated his wife . . . When the general made the soldiers and the persons who were with him come together, the Indian did not recognize the man, . . . but he said that he could tell the horse, because he had held his bridle, and so he was taken to the stables, and found the horse, and said that the master of the horse must be the man. The man denied doing it, seeing that he had not been recognized, and it may be that the Indian was mistaken in the horse. . . . The next day one of the Mexican Indians who was guarding the horses of the army, came running in, saying that a companion of his had been killed, and that the Indians . . . were driving off the horses towards the villages. The Spaniards tried to collect the horses again, but many were lost, including seven of the general's mules.

If you do not obey us

As he had been ordered by the general (Coronado) not to take them alive but to make an example of them so that other natives would fear the Spaniards, Don Garcia ordered 200 stakes to be prepared at once to burn them alive. Nobody told him about the peace that had been granted, for the soldiers knew as little as he, and those who would have told him about it remained silent, not thinking that it was any of their business. Then when the enemies saw that the Spaniards were binding them and beginning to roast them, about a hundred men who were in the tent began to struggle and defend themselves with . . . the stakes they could seize. Our men who were on the floor attacked the tent on all sides . . . and then the horsemen chased those who escaped. As the country was level, not a man remained alive, unless it was some who remained hidden in the village and escaped that night to spread throughout the country the news that the strangers did not respect the peace they had made. . . .

Editor's Note: That harsh winter, the Spaniards, according to Casteñeda, went along the roads telling the Indians to "make peace and telling them they would be pardoned and might consider themselves safe, to which they replied that they did not trust those who did not know how to keep good faith once they had been given it, . . . and that they did not keep their word when they burned those who surrendered in the village." Forced to give up their food supplies to the Spaniards, weakened by ongoing combat, humiliated by friars who forced Catholicism upon them, the gentle Tigues made one last desperate attempt to defend their villages. Casteñeda records what happened.

As they paid no attention to the demands made on them except by shooting arrows from the upper stories with loud yells, and would not hear of peace, Don Garcia Lopez de Cardenas returned to his companions who had left to keep up the attack on Tiguex. A large number of those in the village came out and our men rode off slowly, pretending to flee, so that they drew the enemy on to the plain, and then turned on them and caught several of the leaders. Then . . . the general ordered the army to go and surround the village. . . . They began the siege; but as the enemy had had several days to provide themselves with stores, they threw down such quantities of rocks upon our men that many of them were laid out, and they wounded nearly a hundred with arrows, several of whom afterward died. . . . The siege lasted fifty days, during which time several assaults were made. The lack of water was what troubled the Indians most. They dug a very deep well inside the village, but were not able to get water, and while they were making it, it fell in and killed 30 persons. Two hundred of the besieged died in the fights. . . .

One day, before the capture was completed, they asked to speak to us, and said that, since they knew we would not harm the women and children, they wished to surrender their women and sons, because they were using up their water. It was impossible to persuade them to make peace, as they said the Spaniards would not keep an agreement made with them. So they gave up

Conquistadores, 1540 (1927)
Anders John Haugseth

Zuwang, Pecos, at Taos
(circa 1902)
Kenneth Chapman

about a hundred persons, women and boys, who did not want to leave them. . . .

Fifteen days later they decided to leave the village one night, and did so, taking the women in their midst, . . . but they were driven back with great slaughter until they came to the river, where the water flowed swiftly and very cold. They threw themselves into this, and as the men had come quickly to assist the cavalry, there were few who escaped being killed or wounded. . . . They brought these back, cured them, and made servants of them. . . . The soldiers left the ambuscade and went to the village and saw the people fleeing. They pursued and killed large numbers of them. At the same time those in the camp were ordered to go over the town, and they plundered it, making prisoners of all the people who were found in it, amounting to about a hundred women and children. This siege ended the last of March. . . . The 12 villages of Tiguex, however, were not repopulated at all during the time the army was there, in spite of every promise of security that could be given to them.

Editor's Note: The Spaniards continued to rape, murder, pillage, and starve every other Pueblo Indian tribe in New Mexico for the next 140 years, until the people revolted in 1680, driving out the Spaniards and destroying their churches and artifacts. Until the Spaniards returned in 1693, the Indians tried to go back to the old ways, but it was already too late.

A Tewa elder speaks of the revolt, 1680

(In response to an interrogation by Governor Otermin, an aged Southern Tewa man, captured on the road near Socorro, spoke through an interpreter to the fleeing Spaniards.)

For a long time, because the Spanish punished sorcerers, the nation of the Tewas, Taos, Picuris, Pecos, and Jemez had been plotting to rebel and kill the Spaniards and the religious, and that they had been planning constantly to carry it out down to the present occasion . . . He declared that the resentment which all Indians have in their hearts has been so strong, from the time this kingdom was discovered, because the religious and the Spaniards took away their idols and forbade their sorceries and idolatries; that they have inherited from their old men the things pertaining to the ancient customs; and that he has heard this resent-ment spoken of since he was of an age to understand.

Pedro de Casteñeda

THE ROCK

After early Mass the next morning Father Latour and his guide rode off across the low plain that lies between Laguna and Acoma. In all his travels the Bishop had seen no country like this. From the flat red sea of sand rose great rock mesas, generally Gothic in outline, resembling vast cathedrals. They were not crowded together in disorder, but placed in wide spaces, long vistas between. This plain might once have been an enormous city, all the smaller quarters destroyed by time, only the public buildings left, piles of architecture that were like mountains. The sandy soil of the plain had a light sprinkling of junipers, and was splotched with masses of blooming rabbit brush, that olive-colored plant that grows in high waves like a tossing sea, at this season covered with a thatch of bloom, yellow as gorse, or orange like marigolds.

This mesa had an appearance of great antiquity, and of incompleteness; as if with all the materials for world-making assembled, the Creator had desisted, gone away and left everything on the point of being brought together, on the eve of being arranged into mountain, plain, plateau. The country was still waiting to be made into a landscape.

Ever afterward the Bishop remembered his first ride to Acoma as his introduction to the mesa country. One thing which struck him at once was that every mesa was duplicated by a cloud mesa, like a reflection, which lay motionless above it or moved slowly up from behind it. These cloud formations seemed to be always there, however hot and blue the sky. Sometimes they were flat terraces, ledges of vapor; sometimes they were dome-shaped, or fantastic, like the tops of silvery pagodas, rising one above another, as if an oriental city lay directly behind the rock. The great tables of granite set down in an empty plain were inconceivable without their attendant clouds, which were a part of them, as the smoke is part of the censer, or the foam of the wave.

All this plain, the Bishop gathered, had once been the scene of a periodic man-hunt; these Indians, born in fear and dying by violence for generations, had at last taken this leap away from the earth, and on that rock had found the hope of all suffering and tormented creatures—safety. They came down to the plain to hunt and to grow their crops, but there was always a place to go back to. If a band of Navajos were on the Acoma's trail, there was still one hope; if he could reach his rock—Sanctuary! On the winding stone stairway up the cliff, a handful of men could keep off a multitude. The rock of Acoma had never been taken by a foe but once, by Spaniards in armor. It was very different from a mountain fastness; more lonely, more stark and grim, more appealing to the imagination. The rock, when one came to think of it, was the utmost expression of human need; even mere feeling yearned for it; it was the highest comparison of loyalty in love and friendship. Their rock was an idea of God, the only thing their conquerors could not take from them.

Already the Bishop had observed in Indian life a strange literalness, often shocking and disconcerting. The Acomas, who must share the universal human yearning for something permanent, enduring, without shadow of change, they had their ideas in substance. They actually lived upon their Rock; were born upon it and died upon it. There was an element of exaggeration in anything so simple!

As they drew near the Acoma mesa, dark clouds began boiling up from behind it, like ink spots spreading in a brilliant sky. They stopped just west of the pueblo a little before sunset, a pueblo very different from all the others the Bishop had visited; two large communal houses, shaped like pyramids, gold-colored in the afternoon light, with the purple mountain lying just behind them.

Gold-colored men in white burnooses came out on the stairlike flights of the roofs, and stood still as statues, apparently watching the changing light on the mountain. There was a religious silence over the place; no sound at all but the bleating of goats coming home through clouds of golden dust.

These two houses, the Padre told him, had been continuously occupied by this tribe for more than a thousand years. Coronado's men found them there, and described them as a superior kind of Indian, handsome and dignified in bearing, dressed in deerskin coats and trousers like those of Europeans.

ANGLO INTRUSION

With the United States' annexation of New Mexico in the nineteenth century came yet another religion and foreign customs. More of our land was taken away, drastically reducing our resources. In spite of the fact that many people from our village served heroically in World War II, we were not given the right to vote until 1948. We still perform our military obligations with pride. We remain skeptical about religious beliefs other than our own. We are concerned about Anglo intrusion.

Anonymous
Jemez State Monument

Though the mountain was timbered, its lines were so sharp that it had the sculptured look of naked mountains like the Sandias. The general growth on its sides was evergreen, but the canyon and ravines were wooded with aspens, so that the shape of every depression was painted on the mountain–side, light green against the dark, like symbols; serpentine, crescents, half–circles. This mountain and its ravines had been the seat of old religious ceremonies, honeycombed with noiseless Indian life, the repository of Indian secrets, for many centuries.

The weather alternated between blinding sand storms and brilliant sunlight. The sky was as full of motion and change as the desert beneath, it was monotonous and still, and there was so much sky, more than at sea, more than anywhere else in the world. The plain was there, under one's feet, but what one saw when one looked about was that brilliant blue world of stinging air and moving cloud. Even the mountains were mere ant–hills under it. Elsewhere the sky is the roof of the world; but here the earth was the floor of the sky.

Willa Cather

Cliff-perched Acoma (1904)
Edward S. Curtis

THE KIVA

The Kiva, a circular room without windows, could be entered only by the square opening in the roof, at once a smoke hole and a doorway. This was the meeting place for the men of the clan, but it was more than that. In it, Salt and boys of his own age, and boys before his time, were taught the art and skills of manhood. History and legend were told here, and the manner in which a man should stand before the world was proclaimed in many long speeches.

The interior was not entirely dark, since a fan of light came from above and a bed of red coals in the fire pit near the center of the room produced a faint glow, but it was so dim that Salt stood with one hand on the ladder until his eyes would save him from colliding with people. A knot of older men sat in a tight ring near the fire pit. They were passing a short–stemmed pottery pipe from one to another, each man puffing four times, then twice more, then handing it on.

As his eyes adjusted themselves and Salt could make his way to the seat as-signed to him, his mind reached out to the men, his fathers, whose hands had

Harvest Dance (1976)
J. D. Roybal

worked so cleverly to lay together the stones for these walls. Men talked of kinship, but the laying up of a wall for one's children to use was a real thing. It bridged and held together those who had gone on and those who remained, in everlasting kinship. Salt always felt this when he looked upon the walls of his kiva.

Against the outer wall, at even intervals, six pillars reached to the top like six strong men and supported the pine beams on which the roof rested. In between these pillars ran a waist–high bench of stone. Those who sat on the bench were elevated above others, hence the seats were reserved for certain officers called "Speakers."

In the south wall of the kiva a square hole just above the floor brought fresh air. A slab of stone standing upright between the fresh–air opening and the fire pit deflected the current of air and caused it to circulate around the room and to create a draft for the fire. The walls were whitewashed frequently, as Salt and the other young men knew, since they performed the work. Once a year, when the clan leaders prepared for the Earth Renewing ceremony, the leader of the Masked God society repainted the sacred symbols on the facing side of the stone pillars.

The men who had been smoking near the center of the room presently rose and moved to their seats on the benches. The talk would begin. Speaking in the kiva followed a regular procedure. Each of the principal officers had a spokesman to talk for him. Sometimes a spokesman came to a situation when he did not know what his man wanted said, and in that case the meeting might break up, or others might change the subject.

As the meeting began, Salt's attention wandered. From thinking of ancient kinship with his fathers, his mind had skipped to his morning run and he was again chasing a rabbit through the sagebrush in the half–light. A man had duties to perform, and meeting in the kiva was one of the ways in which a man fulfilled himself. But the boy could still remind the man that nothing in the world was as pleasant as running free and alone in a great space, when the stars are dimming and soft winds rise in the west!

D'Arcy McNickle
Flathead

TAOS PUEBLO, 1882

Editor's Note: This is one of the first descriptions of Taos Pueblo. The etchings are among the earliest efforts to depict Pueblo Indian life.

In front of the North Pueblo stands a row of huge bake–ovens, conical in shape, each provided with a large door and a hole for the draft. Most of the year they are unused, save by the dogs, who find them snug kennels at night, or by the pet eagles for whom the dome–tops seem to have a peculiar fascination. Reaching the walls of the structure, twenty yards farther back, we mount one of the many ladders and gain the first platform. The door which first confronts us is about half a man's height, and stooping, we enter. After a moment the eye becomes accus-

A Taos Pet (1883)
Peter Moran

tomed to the dim light of the apartment, and we glance about. The room probably measures fifteen feet by twenty feet, with a height of seven and a half feet. In one corner is the open fireplace, about which lie pots, large and small, used in cooking, a pile of piñon branches and mesquit roots for fuel, and a large olla with open mouth serving as a deposit for ashes. Along one side is the bed, with its cushion of skins and blankets, under which are concealed the few valuables of the occupant. From the rafters hangs the cradle, a stout wicker basket furnished with soft skins, and beside it are strung festoons of many–colored ears of corn, red peppers, jerked meat, bear grass, feathers, etc.

A multitude of ladders of all sizes, charred and cracked chimneys, surmounted by bulky caps; a bake–oven large enough for a night's lodging, trap–doors *ad infinitum*, poles of odd and unnecessary lengths, which serve, as occasion requires, for jerking meat and drying clothes, are what confront us on each exit from the dim dwellings into the intense sunlight. As we mount higher the walls become more delicate and the ceilings lower, the highest story of the North Pueblo barely accommodating a person in sitting posture. The owner sleeps inside, but lives, so to speak, on his front porch. Here and there, on a balcony by itself, is a large wooden cage, which indicates ownership in an eagle, though usually the bird, with wings clipped, is descried enjoying his probatory freedom on an isolated clothes–pole, or in the lofty summit of a tree of the sacred grove.

Henry R. Poore

OATH OF OFFICE OF THE PUEBLOS

Into your care we entrust our land and our people. Regardless of whether you are poor, or lack the oratory to express yourself fluently, you will to the best of your ability be the protector, impartially, for your people. The stranger who comes into our land will become as one of your people, regardless of race, color or creed, and you will give unto them the same protection and rights as you would your own. You will cherish and protect all that contains life, from the lowliest crawling creatures to the human. By hasty word or deed you will refrain from hurting the feelings, both mentally and physically, of your people. In times when you, to the best of your ability and judgment, have resorted to every means to correct an individual who through stubbornness remains contrary to the point of disrespect for the office you hold and would through his action be a bad example to his fellow man, you will question him four times whether he will continue to set aside peaceful, intelligent reasoning. If his answer is "yes," the four times, then you may strike him with the fist of your hand, and four times, if necessary.

Joe S. Sando
Jemez

THE ANCIENT STRENGTH

I had never before attended a tribal council. In the case of San Leandro, I would be encountering the ages–old theocracy, for which the lay officials are a front. I was curious and a trifle excited, and more than ordinarily aware of impressions, as I entered the village Wednesday morning and came into the large rectangular plaza, entering at the northwest corner, by the Catholic church, which, with its two low towers, rises a little above the other buildings. The plaza is an expanse of hard–trampled, clayey earth, dusty in dry weather, with nothing growing in it but one splendid cottonwood near the middle of the south side. The flat–roofed houses—some one story, some two stories high, some with porches—form a nearly solid enclosure. The native adobe is a warm brown with a slight sparkle to it, and under the porches—in New Mexico they are called by the Spanish name, *portale*—the walls are usually whitewashed. There is variation in the size of the houses, in the arrangement of doors, and in the windows, which range from tiny prehistoric apertures to modern metal casements. The whole, though uniformly composed of rectangles, is not at all monotonous. Adobe weathers into softness and the Indians build largely by eye, so that angles are not quite true and the most regular construction achieves naturally the irregularity that the Greeks used to plan for.

In front of the houses and the close to them there are altogether eight *hornos*, the beehive–shaped ovens, standing about four feet high, that the Spanish introduced. They are the only curved surfaces; there are no arches. One of the much touted charms of adobe is how it takes sunlight and shadow, the sunlight absorbed and softened, the shadow luminous. The play of light and shadow around a plaza such as this is principal beauty. On the hornos, the light blending into shade over the curves is a delicate and wonderful thing.

An Indian plaza is bare, harmonious, and snug. On an off afternoon such as that Wednesday, there will be some children playing in it, a few mongrels taking the sun, and in front of one or two houses pottery and other wares, usually tended by a girl, set out in the hope of tourists. Even with the children and dogs, the village seems empty. Tourists are disappointed not to see Indians in costume all over the place. On ordinary days, the men are busy in the fields—unless they

are in the kiva working up a ceremony—and the women are at their housework or pottery–making. There's no reason why anybody should be around, and when you come to think of it, how is it that even in quite small non–Indian settlements so many people seem to have business on the streets? What keeps them going to and fro? Hanged if I know.

I said that a Pueblo plaza is snug. You could also say contained, almost forti-fied. When you work in the ruins the Old People left, you keep trying to project yourself, and one of the things you feel is this enclosed, self–contained quality, whether it's in a cliff dwelling jammed onto a high ledge of rock in the Navajo country or a little, open site near the Rio Grande. The same thing is present in the pueblos of today, and it goes back at least to Basket Maker III, a dozen centuries or so ago; we don't know how they placed their dwellings before that. The houses and the people, few or many, stand close together, and perhaps that's why they are still here after a couple of thousand years of droughts and crop failures, of Navajos, Apaches, Comanches, Utes, and the white man.

Oliver La Farge

REMEMBERING TEWA PUEBLO HOUSES AND SPACES

Santa Clara Pueblo was a wonderful place to grow up. I was a child there in the 1940's and remember the incredible sense of well-being and containment—both socially and physically. From the plaza or bupingeh (literally, the middle-heart place) of the pueblo, we could see the far mountains encircled our lives and place. Those mountains not only defined the far boundaries of our world but also were where the primary drama of our lives—the growing of clouds and the bringing of that movement and water—was initiated. We continually watched those mountains to see the clouds form out of them and to know on which of their valleys or summits the sun would rise or set. Those mountains, or world boundaries, were far away and were the province of the men and boys who went to visit the shrines there, and who would bring back the spirit and energies of the deer, bear, ram and evergreen plants to blend with ours in the dances and ceremonies of the middle-heart place.

The spaces between those mountains and the pueblo were shared by everyone (men and women, boys and girls). They included the low hills and small canyons where coyotes, rabbits and squirrels lived and where roots, herbs and other ground plants were found. There also were the fields and the large flowing water (the *Posongeh* or Rio Grande) which snaked along the base of the Black Mesa. The Black Mesa included the cave that went down into the center of the earth and was the home of the *Tsavejo* or the masked whippers. There were dark areas, such as the cave, and light areas, such as the top of the low hills, from which we could see the far mountains of the four directions and a large part of the north-south valley within which lay the Posongeh and the pueblo.

As the pueblo, or human space, was encircled by high mountains, low hills and flat fields, the center point (*nansipu*), from which the people emerged out of the underworld, was also girdled by different spaces within the pueblo. The nansipu, marked by an inconspicuous stone, was located within the middle-heart place, or the plaza. The plaza was bounded by house structures, which in turn were encircled by the corrals or places where horses, pigs and chickens lived. Beyond that, or sometimes overlapping, were the trash mounds. The trash mounds flowed into the fields, and from there the energy moved into the hills and mountains where it entered those far shrines, moved through the underworld levels or existences and re-emerged through the nansipu.

The stories of the old people told us that we came to live on this fourth level of existence with the help of plants, birds and other animals. Once we emerged out of the underworld, we continued to need those other living beings. In order to find the center point, or the nansipu, the water spider and the rainbow were consulted. Water Spider spread its legs to the north, west, south and east and determined the middle of this world. Then, to make sure that Water Spider was right, Rainbow spread its arch of many colors to the north, west, south and east and confirmed Water Spider's center point. There, the people placed a stone, and around that stone was defined the middle-heart place. Next, the living and sleeping structures were built in terraced forms, like mountains, with stepped tiers which enclosed and protected the plaza, or the valley of the human place.

The house and kiva structures also emulated the low hills and mountains in

A San Juan Farmhouse
(1925)
Edward S. Curtis

their connectedness to the earth. The adobe structures flowed out of the earth, and it was often difficult to see where the ground stopped and where the structures began. The house structures were, moreover, connected to each other, enclosing an outdoor space from which we could directly connect with the sky and focus on the moving clouds. Connectedness was primary. The symbolic flowed into the physical world as the nansipu where the *po–wa–ha* (the breath of the cosmos) flowed out of the underworld into this world.

The kiva structure was totally symbolic. Its rooftop was like the pueblo plaza space from where we could connect with the sky, while the rooftop opening took us into the kiva structure which was like going back into the earth via the nansipu in the plaza. Within the feminine dark interior, the plaza–space configuration was repeated with the human activity area around a nansipu, the earth floor under and the woven–basket roof above, representing the sky. The connecting ladder made of tall spruce or pine trees stood in the middle near the nansipu. Everything was organized to remind us constantly of the primary connections with the earth, sky, other life forms and the cosmic movement. These primary connections were continually reiterated.

The materials used for construction were also symbolically important. In the Rio Grande area, most of the building was with adobe—mud mixed with either ashes or dried plant material. In the Tewa language, the word for "us" is *nung*, and the word for the "earth" or "dirt" is also *nung*. As we are synonymous with and born of the earth, so are we made of the same stuff as our houses.

As children, we tasted houses because of their varying textures and tastes. Not only could houses be tasted, they were also blessed, healed and fed periodically. Before the actual construc-

Woman baking bread
Awa Tsireh

tion of a house, offerings were placed at its four corners. Later, during the housebuilding, prayers would be said, and more offerings were placed within walls and ceiling beams to bless and protect the completed whole. Thereafter, the structure was blessed and fed cornmeal during specific ceremonies. Houses were also given the ultimate respect of dying. During my childhood, when I walked back and forth between the pueblo and the Bureau of Indian Affairs' school, which was about one-half mile away, I would meander among the pueblo structures tasting them. One day, I noticed a crack forming in the wall of a particularly good-tasting house. I watched the crack grow over several weeks until I became concerned about the house falling. I asked my great-grandmother why the people who lived in that house were doing nothing about fixing the crack. She shook her finger at me and said that it was not my business to be concerned about whether the house fell down or not; "It has been a good house, it has been taken care of, fed, blessed and healed many times during its life, and now it is time for it to go back into the earth." Shortly afterward, the house collapsed and, in appropriate time, the same materials were reused to build a new structure in the same place. It was not always easy to tell if walls were going up or falling apart.

Not long after that house fell down, my great-grandmother and I stood and watched the house that we lived in slowly, and most elegantly, crumble into a pile. I had watched, again, a crack working its way down the walls as I washed my face in the washbowl. It was a few minutes before I had the presence of mind to grab my great-grandmother's hand and pull her out of the door before the house collapsed.

Rina Swentzell
Santa Clara

A SNAKE TALE

When I was a youth of about fourteen I herded my father's cattle. It was in the month of August, and just after midday. Going down an arroyo I saw a track as if someone had been dragging a heavy log. Some small bushes were broken. I followed it to see who was dragging this log. It was so strange that the track was not in a straight line. I went up on a small hillock to see where the other cattle were, and I was just about to jump down the slope on the other side, when I saw in front of me on an overhanging rock a very large snake. I could not run. It was coiled. It had an arrow-head mark on the back of its head and smaller ones on its body. Its head was raised. It did not rattle. It seemed a long time before I could jump back and run home to tell my father and uncle. They did not believe me, and would not go back with me to see. A short time after this, a Frenchman was quarrying rock for Samuel Eldbodt, and while he was cooking he heard a sound like a man snoring. He investigated, and in a cave saw a big snake. He killed it. He told my society brother about it, and this is how I know. He brought the snake to Eldbodt, and only one Indian was allowed to see it. This was Luis Kasta, who is now dead. There was no surprise among Indians, only surprise that there could be such a large snake.

San Juan tale, retold by Edward S. Curtis

Snake and sun
Miguel Martinez

A FISH STORY

There occurred in those days a great drought. Rain had not come for many, many days. The crops were dying and the water in the lake was going down and down. Prayers had to be offered to the Great Spirit. This was the duty of the fish people, so they all assembled in the kiva to pray and offer sacrifices to the rain gods.

The custom was to fast and stay in the kiva until the rain came. A woman by the name of Fee–ne–nee was given the duty to feed the fish people, which she did each day at noon. Since the men were fasting, she served them only a small amount of food and a few drops of water.

On the night of the third day, however, one of the men could no longer stand the isolation. When the others went to sleep, he sneaked out of the kiva and ran to a nearby lake. There he drank and drank, swallowing all the water he had been thinking about for three days.

After filling his body with water, he returned to the kiva. He entered slowly and stepped quietly down the stairs so that he would not be heard. Midway between the roof and the floor, however, he burst. Water poured out of his head, eyes, mouth, arms, body, and legs. When this happened, the people who were inside turned into fish, frogs, and all kinds of water animals, and the kiva was filled with water.

The next day at noon, the woman who was in charge of feeding the men went to the kiva. She could not believe what she saw: water was gushing from it straight up into the air, and suspended in the torrent were fish, frogs, eels, snakes, and ducks.

Sadly, with her basket still in her hand, she slowly returned to the village. The first house she visited was that of an untidy old couple. She placed her basket in the center of the room and silently sat by the grinding stone. After making only one stroke of the stone, she too turned into a snake.

Seeing this, the old man and his wife both said, "Something terrible has happened at the kiva." The man ran to find out what as wrong, and at the kiva he saw ducks, beavers, and frogs swimming in the water at the bottom.

The old man knew that this was a bad omen for the people of the village.

When he reached home, he told his wife, "One of the men failed us, and all of them turned into ducks, frogs, eels, snakes, and beavers."

"We can no longer live here," his wife replied. "You must let our people know. We must also make preparations to take this snake, our friend Fee–ne–nee, where she belongs."

The old woman prepared a basket filled with blue cornmeal and placed the little snake inside. Her husband took the basket and headed toward the east, where there was a snake burrow. At the home of the snakes, he fed them blue cornmeal, and one by one all kinds of snakes wiggled through the meal. Then he placed Fee–ne–nee among the others and said to her: "I have brought you to live here. You are now a young lady snake, and with the help of the Great Spirit you will live among your own kind. I give you my blessing."

To the other snakes he said, "I have brought you a sister; take her into your arms."

As the other snakes curled around Fee–ne–nee, the man walked away with tears in his eyes.

At home the old couple cried again and told their people that the law required them to move from their home, O–Ke–owin, and seek another place to live. Now you know why we live where we do. The tragedy that occurred at O–Ke–owin forced our people to move to Xun ochute, which is now San Juan.

San Juan tale, retold by Richard Erdoes and Alfonso Ortiz

OPPOSITE:
*Mo'wa' (Shining Light),
Nambe* (1905)
Edward S. Curtis

AN ACOMA CHILDHOOD

In Deetziyamah, I discovered the world of the Acoma land and people firsthand through my parents, sisters and brothers, and my own perceptions, voiced through all that encompasses the oral tradition, which is ageless for any culture. It is a small village, even smaller years ago, and like other Indian communities it is wealthy with its knowledge of daily event, history, and social system, all that make up a people who have a many–dimensioned heritage. Our family lived in a two–room home (built by my grandfather some years after he and my grand-mother moved with their daughters from Old Acoma), which my father added rooms to later. I remember my father's work at enlarging our home for our grow-ing family. He was a skilled stoneworker, like many other men of an older Pueblo generation who worked with sandstone and mud mortar to build their homes and pueblos. It takes time, persistence, patience, and the belief that the walls that come to stand will do so for a long, long time, perhaps even forever. I like to think that by helping to mix mud and carry stone for my father and other elders I managed to bring that influence into my consciousness as a writer.

Both my mother and my father were good storytellers and singers (as my mother is to this day—my father died in 1978), and for their generation, which was born soon after the turn of the century, they were relatively educated in the American system. Catholic missionaries had taken both of them as children to a parochial boarding school far from Acoma, and they imparted their discipline for study and quest for education to us children when we started school. But it was their indigenous sense of gaining knowledge that was most meaningful to me. Acquiring knowledge about life was above all the most important item; it was a value that one had to have in order to be fulfilled personally and on behalf of his community. And this they insisted upon imparting through the oral tradition as they told their children about our native history and our community and culture and our "stories." These stories were common knowledge of act, event, and be-havior in a close–knit pueblo. It was knowledge about how one was to make a living through work that benefited his family and everyone else.

Because we were a subsistence farming people, or at least tried to be, I learned to plant, hoe weeds, irrigate and cultivate corn, chili, pumpkins, beans. Through counsel and advice I came to know that the rain which provided water was a blessing, gift, and symbol and that it was the land which provided for our lives. It was the stories and songs which provided the knowledge that I was woven into the intricate web that was my Acoma life. In our garden and our corn fields I learned about the seasons, growth cycles of cultivated plants, what one had to think and feel about the land; and at home I became aware of how we must care for each other: all of this was encompassed in an intricate relationship which had to be maintained in order that life continue. After supper on many occasions my father would bring out his drum and sing as we, the children, danced to themes about the rain, hunting, land, and people. It was all that is contained within the language of oral tradition that made me explicitly aware of a yet unarticulated urge to write, to tell what I had learned and was learning and what it all meant to me.

My grandfather was old already when I came to know him. I was only one of his many grandchildren, but I would go with him to get wood for our house–holds, to the garden to chop weeds, and to his sheep camp to help care for his sheep. I don't remember his exact words, but I know they were about how we

A Threshing-Floor at Taos Pueblo (1883)
Henry R. Poore

must sacredly concern ourselves with the people and the holy earth. I know his words were about how we must regard ourselves and others with compassion and love; I know that his knowledge was vast, as a medicine man and an elder of his kiva, and I listened as a boy should. My grandfather represented for me a link to the past that is important for me to hold in my memory because it is not only memory but knowledge that substantiates my present existence. He and the grandmothers and grandfathers before him thought about us as they lived, confirmed in their belief of a continuing life, and they brought our present beings into existence by the beliefs they held. The consciousness of that belief is what informs my present concerns with language, poetry, and fiction.

Simon J. Ortiz
Acoma

PART SIX

HUNTING

THE SECRET TRAIL

It was hard to believe in a secret trail. Salt had been born in a house lying under the cliff and lived all his days scrambling over the rubble of rock, exploring eagles' nests on high crags, hunting rabbits in the flat land above the cliff. He knew the trail that led from the village to the bottom of the canyon and also the trail that twisted and climbed to the upper country. No secret about these, since the people of the village used them every day. It wasn't that he doubted the word of the Holy One, but it was like being told that summer comes twice in a year or that he could enter his own house without going through the opening in the roof.

After leaving the cave house of the Holy One that morning, he spent the entire day alone, stopping at home only long enough to put two handfuls of parched corn in the buckskin bag he carried at his waist. He would find the secret trail, as he had promised, though he would start with a heavy heart. He fled to the flat country above the canyon to begin the search, but most of all to be by himself.

JOSÉ REY TOLEDO

Buffalo hunt
José Rey Toledo
Jemez

For he was troubled. In the course of one day's journey of the sun, he had himself traveled from a boy's concern with the hunting of rabbits to a knowledge of the dangers with which his elders lived. It was a long journey to make in so short a time. His mind had to take it in. His flesh had to find warmth again. He had to learn how to act in a threatening world.

The elders were fond of saying that, if a man expected to find truth, he should seek it alone. Salt was not sure it meant the same thing, but he had discovered that he could think better, and indeed he often felt better, when he went off by himself. On some of his lonely excursions, he thought only of going as far as he could, and he would run and walk by turns, until at a day's end he had passed beyond his known world. Then, if he had killed a rabbit with his throwing stick or snared a bird in his net of woven hair, he would kindle a fire and eat. Or if his running and walking left him too exhausted to hunt, he fed meagerly on parched corn and crawled among warm rocks to sleep. His mother never fretted over these absences; she knew that they were a part of his growing time.

On other excursions, he delighted himself just in looking at things. He might sit on a rock while the sun moved all the way across the sky and watch the comings and goings of a colony of ants. He would shred the tip of a sliver of yucca to make a fine brush, and with a quick paint of saliva and white clay, he would daub the backs of some ants to tell them apart. Then he would smile to himself as he began to understand which ones went out to forage for food, which others labored at hauling grains of sand out of the underground house, and which appeared to act as guards or warriors of the house. It was a fine thing, he thought, just to watch an ant making a world for itself. That was almost as good as running to cover distance and get away from human talk.

That day when Salt went to the flat country above the cliffs, it was to look again at a land that he knew well. The people called it the flat country, but really it was not flat. The earth rose in round hills, with shallow valleys between, or it lay in long ridges out of which an edge of broken brown rocks showed like the teeth of a monster. The low-growing pinion and cedar trees which, close at hand, appeared so green, turned blue-black in the distance. Knife-leaded yucca plants and cholla cactus grew between the trees. The women prized the yucca, because from its roots they made a fine froth in which they washed their hair. In other clear spaces the grass grew thick and made moving patterns in the wind, and the grass was prized by the deer and antelope, whose flashing tails might be seen through the pine trees on almost any day one came up from the canyon.

One breathed freer in this open country. One's fears and doubts, if they were the fears and doubts of a boy growing up, fell away, and one's heart grew light again.

Up here in the flat country were the planted fields from which the Village of the White Rocks drew life and the songs that fill a life. These fields stretched from almost the rim of the canyon to the very point at which the sky came down to the land. Along this entire reach, the earth was quite level, except that it sloped from each side toward the center, as if it had been the bowl of an old lake. The field that belonged to Salt's family was about midway along and toward the low center. Each family placed a boundary of sticks and stones around its plot. Each of the Seven Clans making up the village had its own land, and these lands, too, were marked off and a boundary post gave the sign for the clan.

The fields were never deserted. Even when the cleaning out of the weeds had been completed and the plants had only to grow and fulfill themselves, men

The secret trail
Allan Houser

from the village remained close by. They might be out of sight in a clump of cedar trees, but they were there, watching. Deer liked the tender top growth of corn; ground squirrels were fond of succulent roots; crows waited for the ears to fill. Many walking and crawling animals besides the people of the village waited to feast on the corn, beans, and squash that grew in those fields. An even greater danger, one that folk preferred not to mention, were the hungry peoples who came down from the north, sometimes from the east, and carried off entire crops. They too waited until the ripening time, and when they came, the flat country was filled with fierce shouting and moans and the sounds of clubs and stones striking dully on flesh.

Today, Salt was mindful of the men watching from the trees. He must be careful not to appear to be looking for anything, or they would come and offer to join in the search. He knew how tiresome it became sitting through the day with nothing to do but watch clouds and learn new songs from an elder uncle, and he decided it would be better to act the part of a child at play, wandering aimlessly in the sun. It would be reported in the kiva of course, that he was not performing his duties as he should, and not helping his family. That could not be helped.

In considering the secret trail, he had decided that it was impossible to look for it in the village. It might start from one of the seven kivas, or even from under the floor of a house. Prying into such places was unlikely to accomplish results. But since the trail was planned as an escape to the country above the cliffs, it could be assumed that somewhere up here he would find the other end. That is, if the trail really existed.

He worked out a game of playing eagle; at least anyone watching him from the trees would guess it was that. To play the game, he would find a mound of rocks or a low hill. There he would stand poised, appearing to survey the land stretched below his perch. He would move his head from side to side. Then, with outstretched arms, he would swoop down from his high place and run, not too fast, in long sweeping curves that took him through pine thickets and open spaces, and he would tilt his arms as he turned and peered at the ground. When he pounced for the kill, he would leap high and come down on all fours. That allowed him time to search the mound of earth around a badger hole or to scratch away the brown needles at the base of a pine tree. He hardly knew what he was looking for, but somewhere, if his eyes were sharp he would find a sign, a stray footprint, a worn place in the grass, a marking on a rock, something that would lead him to his goal.

D'Arcy McNickle
Flathead

THE MAN WHO KILLED THE DEER

In the Government office two hundred miles away, there is that Indian lawyer, our mouth in many matters. There is the judge in town, a short walk. Are we to turn this young man alone over to the judge? Or are we to call this Indian lawyer? And what are we to tell him? We must move more evenly together. We must be of one mind, one heart, one body.

Silence spoke, and it spoke the loudest of all.

There is no such thing as a simple thing. One drops a pebble into a pool, but the ripples travel far. One picks up a little stone in the mountains, one of the little stones called Lagrimas de Cristo—and look! It is shaped like a star; the sloping mountain is full of stars as the sloping sky. Or take a kernel of corn. Plant it in Our Mother Earth with the sweat of your body, with what you know of the times and seasons, with your proper prayers. And with your strength and manhood Our Father Sun multiplies and gives it back into your flesh. What then is this kernel of corn? It is not a simple thing.

Nothing is simple and alone. We are not separate and alone. The breathing mountains, the living stones, each blade of grass, the clouds, the rain, each star, the beasts, the birds and the invisible spirits of the air—we are all one, indivisible. Nothing that any of us does affects us all.

So I would have you look upon this thing not as a separate simple thing, but as a stone which is a star in the firmament of earth, as a ripple in a pool, as a kernel of corn. I would have

The Old-Fashioned Deer Hunter
Ralph Martinez

you consider how it fits into the pattern of the whole. How far its influence may spread. What it may grow into . . .

So there is something else to consider. The deer. It is dead. In the old days we all remember, we did not go out on a hunt lightly. We said to the deer we were going to kill, "We know your life is as precious as ours. We know that we are both children of the same Great True Ones. We know that we are all one life on the same Mother Earth, beneath the same plains of the sky. But we also know that one life must sometimes give way to another so that the one great life of all may continue unbroken. So we ask your permission, we obtain your consent to this killing."

Ceremonially, we said this, and we sprinkled meal and corn pollen to Our Father Sun. And when we killed the deer we laid his head toward the East, and sprinkled him with meal and pollen. And we dropped drops of his blood and bits of his flesh on the ground for Our Mother Earth. It was proper so. For then when we too built its flesh into our flesh, when we walked in the moccasins of its skin, when we danced in its robe and antlers, we knew that the life of the deer was continued in our life, as it in turn was continued in the one life all around us, below us and above us.

We knew the deer knew this and was satisfied.

But this deer's permission was not obtained. What have we done to this deer, our brother? What have we done to ourselves? For we are all bound together, and our touch upon one travels through all to return to us again. Let us not forget the deer.

The old Cacique spoke. It is true that the young men nowadays did not observe such proper steps. And it was true that the game was becoming scarce because of it. Was it true that next the water would fail them, the air become dull and tasteless, the life go out of the land?

"So I would have you consider whether it is not time to be more strict with our young men so corrupted with evil modern ways, lest we ourselves dwindle and vanish entirely. This I say," he ended. "Dios knows, will help us, will give us medicine."

Here they were then, all these things and shadows of things ensnared like flies in the web of silence. They fluttered their wings. They shook and distorted the whole vast web. But they did not break free. For it was the web which binds us to the other, and all to the life of which we are an inseparable part—binds us to the invisible shapes that have gone and those to come, in the solidarity of one flowing whole. . . .

Frank Waters

HUNTER'S MORNING

I went out only once with my bow last year
high into the scattered snow mountains above Vallecitos and
did not get a deer but caught the before sunrise chill on my face
felt my weight break the still–frozen snow beneath my feet
looked back to see my prints just visible in the coming light
smelled a cool wetness of clear springs trickling in the dark
saw the outlines of tall ponderosa pine with ice–bent branches
quietly rustling in the wind's soft breathing as I climbed
still higher
stopped to catch my breath and heard two far–off crows caw
for the coming sun and was audience to coyotes barking
back and forth between unseen canyons

Hunting the deer
Emiliana Yepa
Jemez

watched the blue–grey sky lighten and silent stars fade
felt cold Winter breezes numb my face while I sat shivering
on a rocky ledge overlooking a dim and hazy horizon
blew warm breath into my cupped hands and looked and listened
attentive, while the sun, now rising
cast patches of red and yellow light on distant blue mountains
walked as quietly as I could through dry scrub oak thickets
looking for fresh tracks and droppings in the calm splendor of dawn
began to feel that warm flow run all through me
stopped and prayed, whispering gratitude for that one hunter's morning
held in memory

Harold Littlebird
Laguna/Santo Domingo

THE DEER HUNT

In the fall, the Laguna hunters go to the hills and mountains around Laguna Pueblo to bring back the deer. The people think of the deer as coming to give themselves to the hunters so that the people will have meat through the winter. Late in the winter the Deer Dance is performed to honor and pay thanks to the deer spirits who've come home with the hunters that year. Only when this has been properly done will the spirits be able to return to the mountains and be reborn into more deer who will, remembering the reverence and appreciation of the people, once more come home with the hunters.

Leslie Marmon Silko
Laguna

HOW THE DEER GOT THEIR RED EYES

Old Deer Woman and Old Wolf Woman were good friends. They used to go out together after wood and food. One day when they were out gathering wood, both became tired, so they sat down to rest under a juniper tree. Wolf Woman asked Deer Woman to let her comb her hair. When Deer Woman sat down, Wolf Woman hit her and killed her. Then Wolf Woman got some of the meat and took it home to her children. When she was passing the house of Deer Woman's children, she gave them a piece of meat and told them their mother would be late coming home that night. Then the little Deer Children took the piece of meat inside to roast it.

As the children were roasting the meat, it started to talk. The meat said it was their mother's flesh and that Old Wolf Woman had killed her. So the children sat down and cried all night long.

Pecos Bull
Augustine Fragua

Next morning Wolf Woman went out to the mountain to get the rest of her meat. The little Wolf Children and the little Deer Children came out to play together. The Wolf Children told the Deer Children that if they wished to have pretty eyes, too, they knew how to get them. So they took a lot of corn cobs, started a fire, and shut the Wolf Children inside the cave. Then the Deer Children ran away before Old Wolf Woman came back.

When the Wolf Woman returned, she found her two children smothered to death, so she ran after the Deer Children.

The Deer Children ran until they came to a flock of Blackbirds, which they asked to help them escape from Wolf Woman. So the Blackbirds put the children inside of a football and kicked the football down south.

By and by the Wolf Woman came to the Blackbirds and asked them if they had seen the Deer Children run by. The Blackbirds did not answer. Soon the Deer Children came to a river, where they told Beaver to take them across. When Wolf Woman came there, she asked Beaver to take her across.

After the old Wolf Woman got on Beaver's back, he began to dive, and it took a long time to cross the river. By that time the Deer Children had reached the cave where the other Deer were living, and they told the Deer what had happened to their mother.

Then all the male Deer began to sharpen their horns to wait for Wolf Woman. Soon she came. The Deer told her to pass in. The Deer Children were in there. As soon as Wolf Woman came down, the old male Deer caught her on their horns and killed her, and they made soup out of her.

All the Deer were told not to drop any soup on the floor, for if they did so, some Wolf would come out from the den. One of the Deer Children happened to drop some soup on the floor. Whereupon a lot of Wolves came running, and ever since that time wolves and deer have been enemies, and the deer have red eyes because the little Deer Children cried so hard when Old Wolf Woman killed their mother, Old Deer Woman.

Isleta tale, collected by Gene Meany Hodge
from *Kachina Tales from the Indian Pueblos*, Sunstone Press

THE RITUALS OF HUNTING

Many years ago our grandfathers, some of whom were in the Eagle Clan, often went out hunting, bringing back numbers of deer, antelope, and other game that they corralled near a water hole.

When they went out on such parties they came to the water hole, first setting up the corral. The corral had only one opening and just outside of this opening a tent was put up. Alongside the corral, trenches were dug, with twigs and leaves covering them. Further on, out of sight of the corral, the men built a little shed for themselves. Around that, leaves were scattered. Then a hanger was built upon which the deer meat was to be dried. With prayers and sacred rituals, the trappings were blessed. In the corral, another trench was dug where prayersticks would be planted. By the time these projects were set up, the sun was setting, whereupon a paint was prepared that would lure the deer into the surrounding area so the men could easily come upon them. Long prayers and chants followed until they had all been said and sung.

Then the men began preparing the costumes they were to wear. White woven cloth was made into loose trousers and long shirts. That finished, the men retired for the night, anxious to carry on with the hunt.

Early in the morning they awakened and gathered their horses. After eating

Reindeer people
Awa Tsireh

their morning meal, they set out upon horseback into the forest to capture the deer. With the paint mixed the night before, they painted their faces. When they came across a very tall tree, a man took a post upon the tree overlooking the land.

On they went, for some time looking and scouting around. Upon finding a herd of deer, the men split up, usually into two groups of three. They then came at the herd from two directions. With two other men following they approached the herd. Before long, the deer started running back and forth between the groups of men. The two men following made the sounds of another deer and soon the herd headed in the direction of the corral. Swerving back and forth, the deer came in, and by luck and the spirits of the supernatural beings helping, the corral was full of deer.

With brush, blankets, and heavy poles the opening was closed. The leader of the herd then came forward and circled around four times, then with a strong leap, he bounded out of the corral. No one bothered to follow this buck, as it was thought that he had brought his children to their rightful place.

All of the men came, and the one chosen to kill the deer, dressed appropriately, entered the corral armed with a bow and some arrows. He carried out his duty, bringing down each deer until they had all been killed.

Each deer was bound and the men carried these to the shed from the corral; the blood that mixed into the soil was gathered and bundled and put into a large rug and set aside. The corral was roughly cleaned. Upon returning to the shed, the men began to clean the deer and take the skins off. The meat was quartered and some cut up for eating and the rest cut into jerky, thinned, and hung out to dry on the hangers.

By sundown, the men ate and at night again set out to work until all had been finished. Retiring for the night only to catch a few hours sleep, they spread out on the ground.

The next morning, after gathering and feeding the horses, the men ate and dressed once more. With what was left of the paint, they again went out to hunt. Again the deer were sought and again herded into the corral and killed and butchered.

For four days at a time the men of the Eagle Clan went out for the deer. Even though the deer were in abundance, the men would not pass the four days, for they believed it would not be good if they did. They believed if they did so they would lose their eyesight and become totally blind. When their work was finished, the men took down the corrals, the tent, and the shed and filled up the trenches, all with prayer of thanks. If they did not do this, the cattle and sheep that grazed upon the land would not reproduce normally. The livestock would all miscarry and eventually would die off because the prayers that had been said during the preparation of the corrals, the tent, the sheds, and the hangers would come to bring harm to these living animals.

And so with these rituals, the Zuni were sustained. Today the prayers remain with us, but the actual rituals of hunting are no longer practiced. This was the way of the Zuni Eagle clansmen.

The Zuni people, translated by Alvina Quam

PARCHED CORN

When we were children we didn't have any popcorn or anything like that, so they used to roast the blue corn in the ovens, the ovens they make bread in. I must have been maybe eight or nine years old. Because we used to look forward to the time when they'd roast the corn in the oven. And they'd leave the corn overnight. You know, they'd husk the corn, and they'd let it dry, and after it's dry they'd take it off the cob, and then they'd put it out to dry, and then they'd put it in the oven one whole night. After they were finished maybe making bread or something like that, when the oven would be just warm enough to put your corn in. It would be overnight.

And they used to roast it in there, and after we'd take it out we used to be so happy, because we didn't have anything like popcorn or anything, and we used to eat it just like popcorn. And I think that was our most enjoyable time, the time in early autumn, when they used to roast the corn, and we'd look forward to having that corn roasted so we could eat it like popcorn. And today they still eat it and it's called parched corn.

Julia Roybal
San Ildefonso
from *Southwest Indian Cookbook,*
by Marcia Keegan, Clear Light Publishers

ANIMAL DANCE

At sunrise the dancers come down from the hills and are led into the village by the war priests. The buffalo come first, followed by the elk, deer, longhorn sheep and the antelopes. The women go down the road to meet them, and as they pass by, they sprinkle sacred cornmeal on the dancers and ask for blessings.

Most all the pueblos have some kind of a Buffalo dance and they also have a Deer dance, when only the deer participate.

It is a thanksgiving dance, thanking the spirit of the animal of which antler they are wearing and thanking them for giving us food from their flesh.

At the end of the day of dancing, the deer and mountain sheep, the elk and the antelopes are turned loose in the plaza and then the ladies chase them and whoever catches one takes the dancer home and they feed him and give him meat to take home to his family to show appreciation. It is an honor to catch a wild deer.

Pablita Velarde
Santa Clara
from *Southwest Indian Cookbook*, by Marcia Keegan, Clear Light Publishers

Buffalo hunt

THE HUNTING PRAYER

Look at you, magnificent creature lying there,
How is it that we, your poor human brothers,
Could be worthy to borrow
Your life? You honor us, you allow us
To witness the power and magnificence
Of the Creator. God has blessed
Your life and we see that.
Thank God for the continued
Sustenance that is provided
For all our relations:
The sun, the clouds, the rain,
The snow, the water, the air,
The earth and the mystery of fire.
Now we are going to carry
You home; you come with us easily.
Our people will be
Happy to see you.
They will make you welcome.
You will live again
In all our lives, my brother.

Larry Littlebird
Laguna/Santo Domingo

Holy Deer
Larry Littlebird

WHEN I WAS THIRTEEN

When I was thirteen I carried an old .30–30 we borrowed from George Pearl. It was an old Winchester that had a steel ring on its side to secure it in a saddle scabbard. It was heavy and hurt my shoulder when I fired it, and it seemed even louder than my father's larger caliber rifle, but I didn't say anything because I was so happy to be hunting for the first time. I didn't get a deer that year, but one afternoon hunting alone on the round volcanic hill we called Chato, I saw a giant brown bear lying in the sun below the hilltop. Dead or just sleeping, I couldn't tell. I was cautious because I already knew what hours of searching for motion, for the outline of a deer, for the color of a deer's hide can do to the imagination. I already knew how easily the weathered branches of a dead juniper could resemble antlers because I had walked with my father on hunts since I was eight. So I stood motionless for a long time until my breathing was more calm and my heart wasn't beating so hard. I even shifted my eyes away for a moment, hoping to see my uncle Polly or my cousin Richard who were hunting the ridges nearby.

I knew there were no bears that large on Mt. Taylor; I was pretty sure there were no bears that large anywhere. But when I looked back at the slope above me, the giant brown bear was still lying on the sunny slope of the hill above patches of melting snow and tall yellow grass. I watched it for a long time, for any sign of motion, for its breathing, but I wasn't close enough to tell for sure. If it was dead I wanted to be able to examine it up close. It occurred to me that I could fire my rifle over its head, but I knew better than to wake a bear with only a .30–30. All this time I had only moved my eyes, and my arms were getting numb from holding the rifle in the same position for so long. As quietly and as carefully as I probably will ever move, I turned and walked away from the giant bear, still down wind from it. After I had gone a distance down the slope, I stopped to look back to see if it was still a giant brown bear sunning it-self on one of the last warm afternoons of the year, and not just damp brown earth and a lightning–struck log above the snow patches. But the big dark bear remained there, on the south slope of Chato, with its head facing southeast, the eyes closed, motionless. I hurried the rest of the way down the ridge, listening closely to the wind at my back for sounds, glancing over my shoulder now and then.

I never told anyone what I had seen because I knew they don't let people who see such things carry .30–30's or hunt deer with them.

Leslie Marmon Silko
Laguna

Bear and Deer
Justino Herrera

THE BEAR

My grandfather, who was then a young man of 19, went with two of his companions to the sacred Blue Lake to hunt for deer. It was in the early autumn, when the days had become shorter and the afternoons cool in the long shadow of the high forests.

The three young men prepared for the hunt by praying to the spirit of the deer and extending a blessing. They prayed to the deer to not be afraid and to come to them and be their winter food. They danced with deer's antlers tied to their heads, calling the deer's spirit to them.

Then they went, taking very little with them on their backs, because they thought they would be gone from the pueblo only two nights or three nights. Through the wide fields they walked, up the mountain, into the woods that lay all around Blue Lake. They crossed streams and climbed up through thickets. When finally they had come to the edge of Blue Lake, my grandfather left his two young companions and went to look for deer tracks. It was still light but getting on toward early evening.

While the other two were gathering firewood and making camp, my grandfather went off through the trees and into a small meadow. He had his musket with him, but only that. He strode into the tall grass.

Suddenly, he saw something moving, something huge and black. He stopped, but the big black thing started to move quickly toward him. In an instant, before he could take another breath, the bear was upon him. My grandfather was able to push his musket into the side of the bear and pull the trigger.

The gun fired and the bear fell back. But it was still moving, and as a moment passed, the bear stirred, rolled and limped away. My grandfather, even though he was very shaken, followed behind carefully and watched as the bear rolled down a small embankment toward a stream. There the bear gathered up bunches of wet grass and plugged up the hole in his sides where the musket's fireball had gone through.

The bear drank long from the stream and waited. Then it looked up and saw my grandfather reloading his musket. Before my grandfather knew what was happening, the bear was upon him again. This time the bear groaned and mauled my grandfather with sharp claws. Blood flowed from deep cuts all down his arms and his legs. My grandfather fired his musket again into the black bear. The bear took the fireball and fell back, releasing my grandfather.

Now the bear lay on the grass. My grandfather turned and ran, as best he could. He was bleeding all over his body from the bear's attack. He made his way to where his two companions had set up their camp on the shores of Blue Lake.

"We can't stay here," my grandfather told his friends. "I was attacked by a black bear." Then he collapsed. The two companions quickly put together a litter and tied my grandfather to it, and, even though night was coming on, they started down the mountain.

They arrived back at the pueblo. My grandfather was still alive, but very near death. The people cleaned his wounds and laid him down in his house to rest. There, my grandfather slept for many days. A month went by before he was able to speak and move, and another month before he could get on his feet. Winter snows came, and then the first bird songs of spring. My grandfather's gashes had healed and he began to be well again.

For us, the black bear is a holy animal because it carries the power to heal. Little by little my grandfather came back to life. It was because the black bear had embraced him and given him its healing power.

My grandfather was well then, and for the rest of his life from when he was 19 years old, he was strong and vigorous, and he was never ill. And my grandfather lived for many more years, until he died at the age of 125.

Agripito Concha
Taos

HUNTING

I have killed the deer.
I have crushed the grasshopper
And the plants he feeds upon.
I have cut through the heart
Of trees growing old and straight.
I have taken fish from water
And birds from the sky.
In my life I have needed death
So that my life can be.

When I die I must give life
To what has nourished me.
The earth receives my body
And gives it to the plants
And to the caterpillars
To the birds
And to the coyotes
Each in its own turn so that
The circle of life is never broken.

Nancy Wood

The Rabbit Hunter
Oscar Berninghaus

RABBIT HUNT

Many men gathered at the hunt, making the ceremonial circles that honor the earth and its creations, an ancient way on foot, horses and clubs. The way fathers hunted and honored their existence, their muscle, bones, breath. The animal that gives life from the beginning, Deer, Elk, Buffalo, Bear, Trout, Eagle, Rabbit. And we were there where our heart and soul belong. We made our hunt circles on the Indian land. Took a few life forces. Everyone anticipated the better hunt across the road near the hotels and museums. I remember when there was nothing but a few houses—now cars, buildings, people—built on holy hunting grounds. The anticipation left all by the end of the day, sweaty horses, sunburnt runners. Circle after circle, no game, no new life force, the rain clouds never came, the rabbits never came, what prophecy was fulfilled? Why did they pour poison pellets near the big hotels and houses, because they wanted no blood thirsty Savages around when tourists are in abundance, or because they want to control everything? I don't know.

I thought hard about life. There is a limit beyond which man cannot reorganize the earth and sky, to accommodate his needs.

A true hawk swooped fast and low to the ground, a fat groundhog tried hard to scamper into its hole home. A dust cloud arose, wings flapped vigorously, then stopped. True hawk lifted itself up into the sky. Hanging from its talons was the fat ground hog. It flew over me and sang its happy hunting song. A rain of small droplets of blood sprinkled the dirt roof, blood soaked up the dirt around it and a tiny ant got nutrients from the flesh offering and sang, I am sure, its happy hunting song.

Robert Mirabal
Taos

THE PRAIRIE DOGS DANCE

There is a telling that on the mesa Coyote Grandfather lived. He had a little drum, and he used to sit above the road and beat the drum, singing:

"Look out! Look out!
Coyote is going to hit you
On the back, on the back."

Whenever the prairie dogs heard this, they came running. "How beautifully you sing," they teased, and stepped in time to the song.

"Sing again," they pleaded when the old coyote paused to rest.

"Sing again, Coyote Grandfather. It is such fun to dance to your song."

One day, Skunk ran to the prairie–dog village. Old Coyote was dead, he told the little dogs. They must come and see. The prairie dogs thought this was good news if it were true, and they ran out to see for themselves.

There lay old Coyote, stiff upon the ground.

"Let us dance and sing because he is dead and cannot bother us any more," they said.

So they began to dance around Old Coyote and to sing:

"Look out! Look out!
Coyote is going to hit you
On the back, on the back."

Suddenly Old Coyote jumped up and began to strike the prairie dogs down. As he hit each one, Skunk caught it. When there were no more prairie dogs to taunt him, Old Coyote sat back, thinking what a fine meal he would have. But Skunk was nowhere to be seen, and he had made off with all the dogs. That is how it happened that Old Coyote outwitted himself.

Cochiti tale, retold by Evelyn Dahl Reed
from *Coyote Tales from the Indian Pueblos*, Sunstone Press

THE PRIEST'S SON AND THE EAGLE

There lived a little boy with his sister and his parents. They owned many fields where they raised crops. The boy's father was a priest for the people in the village. One morning, when the boy left his home to go to his fields, he walked around his fields and found an eagle's nest. He saw a little eagle in the field and caught it and said to himself that he was going to take the eagle home with him.

When he arrived home he made a house for the eagle and kept it for a pet. His mother asked, "Why are you coming back so early?"

The boy told his mother, "I brought an eagle home and I'm going to keep it." The next day, early in the morning, the boy went out to hunt for food for his eagle. He killed a rabbit and went home. When he went to feed the eagle, it was very pleased with the rabbit and ate it all up.

After that the boy went out to get water for his eagle. By the time he was all finished hunting, it was almost sundown. So he rested for the night. Every day, the little boy kept up with his hunting for his eagle. In the mornings he went hunting for rabbits and in the evenings he got water for his eagle.

While the boy went hunting every day, his father went to work in his fields. The boy had helped his father every day to work in their fields until he found the eagle; then he quit helping his father and started hunting for the eagle. Several days later the little boy's father said to him, "I don't like what you are doing. I'd rather have you help me work in the fields instead of going hunting for rabbits."

The eagle overheard the father and was disappointed. The boy's father wasn't happy when the boy came home with another rabbit. He wanted to feed it to his eagle, but the eagle didn't eat it because he wasn't happy. The boy wondered why the eagle didn't want the rabbit and what had happened to it.

He went to his house to eat supper and after supper he came out to see his eagle again. The rabbit was still where he had left it, and the water was also there. The eagle hadn't eaten the rabbit at all and hadn't drunk the water. So the boy asked his eagle, "Why haven't you eaten or drunk?"

Much to his surprise the eagle talked to the boy and told him why it wasn't happy, that it had overheard the boy's father say that he didn't like for him to go hunting for the eagle. The eagle said, "It is because of you. You haven't been help-ing your father with the crops."

The eagle got angry and asked the boy to let it out of its cage so it could go live someplace else. But the little boy said, "I will go with you."

At first the eagle told him he couldn't go, but the boy insisted that he wanted to go with the eagle. Finally the eagle said, "Okay, you can come with me, but you have to bring some bells with you." So the boy went into his house and got two bells. They were little bells and he put one on each of its legs with a string.

A few minutes later the boy and the eagle flew away together, with the boy sitting on the back of the eagle. At that time the boy's father, mother, and sister were working in their fields. As the two were flying, they flew by his father's fields and saw his parents and sister. So the eagle told the boy to let his parents know that he was going away. So the boy started to sing a song. As he was singing his little sister heard, so she stopped to listen. Once again her brother started to sing. His sister found out that it was her brother singing because as the boy sang, he called out his Indian name. That's why his sister knew that it was her brother singing. Then she told her parents and they all listened. Sure enough, it was their boy singing and telling them that he was going away from home with his eagle.

After the father heard that his boy was going away he wasn't happy, and he was sorry for what he had said about the eagle. But there was nothing he could do. It was too late to stop him. The eagle kept flying with the boy on its back until they reached the eagle's home. When they got there, all of the other eagles were sitting inside of their homes. So the eagle flew in with the boy and greeted the rest of the family.

The eagle family was pleased to see their other eagle coming home, as it had been gone for several days. The eagles noticed that it was bringing a boy home. These eagles weren't like the eagles of today. The eagles, a long time ago, used to turn into people and talk. By their magical ways they changed from eagles to human beings. When they went outside to hunt for food they turned into eagles, but when they stayed inside their houses they were like people. That's why after the boy decided to go with the eagle and live with it and the rest of the eagle family, they made him marry their sister, so he could stay with the eagles.

During the day the boy and his wife stayed home while her brothers went out to hunt for food. Several days later the boy's wife turned herself into an eagle and the boy sat on her back, then they flew out together. As they were hunting they killed a deer. Because the boy's wife and her brothers were eagles they ate their meat raw, but the boy cooked his meat.

Then one day the couple went out together again. Each time when it was time for them to eat, they built a fire together and the boy cooked his meat. His wife always waited for her brothers to come so they could all eat together, but they didn't cook theirs; they ate theirs raw.

As the days went by the wife decided to take him to another place and see their friend. They call their friends their grandfathers and grandmothers. They went to the home of the cranes living on the other side of the mountains. They ate their meals cooked. So when the boy arrived there they fed him deer meat, and it was cooked. The boy stayed with the cranes until it was sundown, then he went back to his wife's place. His wife had gone hunting and later she brought home another deer.

As he went out for a walk each day he met two female hawks. He stayed with them, then he married one of them. There were some witches living on the other side of the mountain. One day when the boy went out for a walk he happened to stop where the witches lived. Later the witches found out that someone had been to their home. They followed the boy until they found him at the home of the eagles. The witches found him and tried to take him. The eagles fed him a spoiled

Mountain Sheep
Chasing the Koshare (1951)
Awa Tsireh

meat, just so the witches wouldn't take him. The boy ate the meat even though it was spoiled, because if the boy didn't eat the meat, the witches would have taken him and killed him so he would become one of them, too.

Finally, the eagle family thought maybe it would be best if he went back to his parents. In the meantime, the boy's father, mother, and little sister were lonesome for him. His sister waited for him every day, hoping he would come home. She used to sit on top of her house by the ladder.

One evening her brother finally came home and the sister saw him coming. She rushed in to tell her parents, but at first they didn't believe her, so she went out again and watched her brother until he came near the house. The parents were so happy to see their boy home again.

Moral: Foolish bravery.

Zuni tale, retold by Frank Hamilton Cushing

A SURE CURE FOR BOTS

I need not tell how the bot-worm gets in a horse's stomach, for every one knows, but I will give you a sure cure if given in time. As soon as a horse's stomach becomes deranged, and the gastric juice not in its normal or natural condition, the worm at once fastens its horns in the walls of the stomach and commences to eat its way out, and in bad cases, upon opening the horse's stomach, you will find the worms in regimental rows stuck as fast to the walls of the stomach as a fish hook in flesh. Now there is common sense in all things. I will now tell you how to overcome the deadly worm. Take a quart of sweet milk and a pint of molasses, and two ounces of laudanum. Mix together and give it blood warm. The worms will let go and drink the sweet drink, and the laudanum will make them all dead drunk in one-half hour. Then give six ounces of aloes dissolved in half gallon of warm water, and while the worms are all drunk they will be carried off through the bowels, and the horse will get well.

J. I. Lighthall

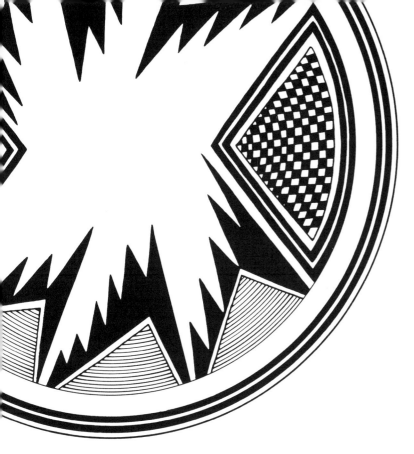

PART SEVEN

CEREMONY
& COURTSHIP

IMPRISONED BY BEARS

This is the story told by Nan–a–tchi–le, or Bird–on–Tree.

Once on a time, a long time ago, a woman was walking in the woods, carrying the babe that was to be born to her, and very happy she was in the lovely evening air and glow of the sun's farewell radiance.

Suddenly a great bear stood before her and the woman was frightened. She tried to run, but the bear caught her in his strong arms and carried her to his cave. There she saw another bear, even larger than the first, and was terribly frightened, but the bears put her on a soft bed of dried grass and skins and did not hurt her. They were very friendly and endeavored to show their good will by giving her food and trying in every way to make her comfortable. But for all their kindness the woman was too frightened to sleep that night. She lay mourning for her people, who were perhaps even then looking for her, and jumped at every movement of her captors, fearful lest they should devour her in the darkness.

Bear and paw prints
M. Coloque

THE IMPORTANCE OF CIGARETTES

In my studies in New Mexico I have been much interested in the sacred smoke. It recurs everywhere. There is hardly a folk–story among the Pueblo Indians in which it does not figure prominently. Not a prayer is offered nor a ceremonial conducted without its aid. But for it the land would be burned up with drought, and the population harpied away bodily by evil spirits. No one thinks of being born or dying without the intervention of the cigarette, and to all the intermediate phases of life it is equally indispensable.

Charles F. Lummis

Next morning she watched the bears and when they both prepared to leave the cave her heart grew lighter as she hoped to run away during their absence. The big fellows lumbered out, one behind the other, but when the second had passed through the opening, they rolled a huge stone before the entrance to her prison. When they were gone the woman tried to push the stone away but could no more move it than she could push out the side of the cave. She then lay on her comfortable bed and wept until she heard the owners of the cave returning. She sat up, listened with all her might and watched light come into the cave as they rolled the stone away. The bears entered and threw a deer before her, indicating that she was to take a share of the prey before they satisfied their own hunger.

Day followed day and the bears were always friendly, but refused to allow their prisoner to depart, rolling up the rock every time they went from the cave. The woman always endeavored to push the barrier away when she was left alone but it would never yield to her feeble strength.

One day when the bears returned the woman's child had come to relieve her loneliness, but it was a strange babe and the bears laughed great bear laughs of pleasure because it was half human and half bear. When they looked at the human side it looked like the woman's own child but when they saw only the bear side it seemed like their cub and they fondled it in bear fashion.

If these shaggy captors had been vigilant about keeping their prisoner before, they doubled their vigilance now because they loved this human–bear child that had been born in their cave. The woman and her child never lacked food—deer, sheep, hares, honey, vegetables, fruit—and they were furnished such other comforts as the bears could give, so they led a fairly comfortable existence. But the woman was weary of the cave and longed to go to her people in the village where she had been born and spent her girlhood, the village where her beloved husband and parents lived. She had ceased to try to push away the stone but every day prayed to Nam–be Que'–o, the Great Mother God, to send rescue.

The bear–boy grew rapidly and played alike with his mother and the bears. As he developed, his mother taught him her language and made known to him her grief, which he finally accepted as his grief also. He learned to pray to the great Father, Nam–bi'quo, and the Great Mother, Nambe Queo, and joined his mother in her prayers for deliverance. As his strength increased he began to try it on the great barrier before their door. For years it was as though he tried to move a mountain, but one day, when he was about half grown, he exclaimed, "Mother, I think the stone moved a little! Nambiquo is about to answer our prayers."

She embraced him with rapture but warned him to be cautious and try his strength on big rocks in their cave until he could be so sure of his power that he could not fail. "If you try to move the stone and are caught," she said, "or if you move it only enough for them to see what you have been doing, the bears will either kill us or guard us so carefully that there will never be a chance for es-cape."

So the bear–boy was cautious. He learned all he could from his mother while the bears were away and learned what he could outside his cave when the bears were home and allowed their prisoners to exercise and get fresh air in the clear-ing outside the cave. Of course this was always done under their watchful eyes and restraining big paws.

And now strength was added to the bear–boy every day. His mother was so astonished at his growth that she thought he must be endowed by the gods themselves. When the bears were home he was careful not to show how much strength he had, but when they were gone, he flung about the boulders in their cave until his mother would almost scream from terror.

A day came when he said, "It is time for me to try my strength and prove that our prayers to the Great Father and Mother have not been in vain."

So he advanced to the front of the cave and began to push against the barri-cading rock. At first it still seemed like the side of the cavern. But the bear–boy continued to strain and push, to rest and to push again. Then, joy to their spirits, the rock creaked, moved, moved again, and finally fell away!

In all the years the mother had been in the prison home, she had never seen sunlight flood the cave except when the bears themselves had rolled the rock away. And now at first when she saw the light she thought the bears must be outside. But soon she knew that her own child had moved the great stone, and at once she was feverish to get away before the bears should return. How furious they would be that the cave had been opened! She remembered the direction of her home and she and the bear–boy ran with all swiftness, often looking behind to see if they were followed.

When they had gone about a mile the mother exclaimed, "They are pursuing us!" and stopped quite still in her terror. The bear–boy looked back and felt his own heart thump with fright, but seizing his mother he ran even swifter with his burden than he had before.

On and on he went until the edge of the mesa that stood before his mother's village was reached. He was now tired, but his strength endured. He climbed the mesa, crossed it, and descended its other side, reaching in safety the village, to be met by a crowd of wondering Indians.

The woman made herself known to her people and they were rejoiced to see her, for they had thought her dead. The strange bear–boy did not please them at first but when they found out that he knew their language and worshipped the Great Nambiquo and Nambe Queo, they took him into their community and he became one of them.

The bear–boy led the men of the pueblo to the haunts of the two bears. There the hunters found them and slew them. Their skins were taken back to the pueblo and nightly the bear–boy and his mother slept upon the furs of the great beasts who had kept them prisoners so many years.

Tewa tale, retold by Ahlee James

OH SWEET HER

beneath a forgotten pine tree
a drum echos
and the songs fade into the rain
it is the last dance
before morning

a dozen hearts away from me
somewhere nervous eyes lurk
waiting to be picked up
dancing nearer and nearer

fog creeps down the valley
and i must stop
before my mind wanders
over to her camp
because she never had long hair . . .

Grandmother
before i learned to crawl
like an aspen leaf
and flew away
from my open arms . . .

Joseph L. Concha
Taos
from *Chokecherry Hunters and Other Poems*, Sunstone Press

Acoma Birds (1977)
Helen Hardin
Santa Clara

DEER HUNTER AND WHITE CORN MAIDEN

Long ago in the ancient home of the San Juan people, in a village whose ruins can be seen across the river from present-day San Juan, lived two magically gifted young people. The youth was called Deer Hunter because even as a boy, he was the only one who never returned empty-handed from the hunt. The girl, whose name was White Corn Maiden, made the finest pottery, and embroidered clothing with the most beautiful designs, of any woman in the village. These two were the handsomest couple in the village, and it was no surprise to their parents that they always sought one another's company. Seeing that they were favored by the gods, the villagers assumed that they were destined to marry.

And in time they did, and contrary to their elders' expectations, they began to spend even more time with one another. White Corn Maiden began to ignore her pottery making and embroidery, while Deer Hunter gave up hunting, at a time when he could have saved many of his people from hunger. They even began to forget their religious obligations. At the request of the pair's worried parents, the tribal elders called a council. This young couple was ignoring all the traditions by which the tribe had lived and prospered, and the people feared that angry gods might bring famine, flood, sickness, or some other disaster upon the village.

But Deer Hunter and White Corn Maiden ignored the council's pleas and drew closer together, swearing that nothing would ever part them. A sense of doom pervaded the village, even though it was late spring and all nature had unfolded in new life.

Then suddenly White Corn Maiden became ill, and within three days she died. Deer Hunter's grief had no bounds. He refused to speak or eat, preferring to keep watch beside his wife's body until she was buried early the next day.

For four days after death, every soul wanders in and around its village and seeks forgiveness from those whom it may have wronged in life. It is a time of unease for the living, since the soul may appear in the form of a wind, a disembodied voice, a dream, or even in human shape. To prevent such a visitation, the villagers go to the dead person before burial and utter a soft prayer of forgiveness. And on the fourth day after death, the relatives gather to perform a ceremony releasing the soul into the spirit world, from which it will never return. But

Deer Hunter was unable to accept his wife's death. Knowing that he might see her during the four–day interlude, he began to wander around the edge of the village. Soon he drifted farther out into the fields, and it was here at sundown of the fourth day, even while his relatives were gathering for the ceremony of release, that he spotted a small fire near a clump of bushes.

Deer Hunter drew closer and found his wife, as beautiful as she was in life and dressed in all her finery, combing her long hair with a cactus brush in preparation for the last journey. He fell weeping at her feet, imploring her not to leave but to return with him to the village before the releasing rite was consummated. White Corn Maiden begged her husband to let her go, because she no longer belonged to the world of the living. Her return would anger the spirits, she said, and anyhow, soon she would no longer be beautiful, and Deer Hunter would shun her.

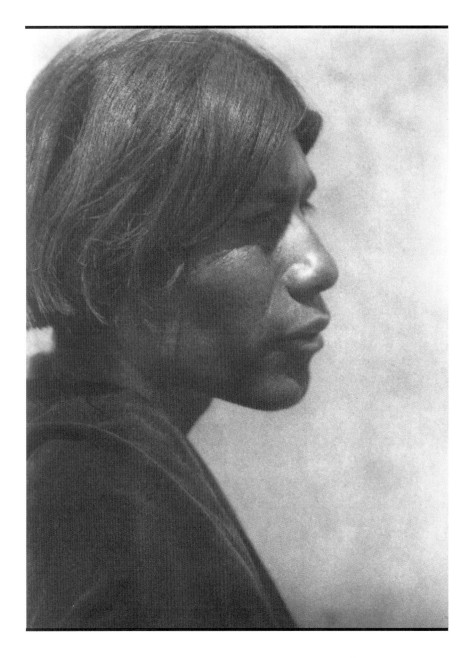

Sotsona (Fox), Santo Domingo (1925)
Edward S. Curtis

He brushed her pleas aside by pledging his undying love and promising that he would let nothing part them. Eventually she relented, saying that she would hold him to his promise. They entered the village just as their relatives were marching to the shrine with the food offering that would release the soul of White Corn Maiden. They were horrified when they saw her, and again they and the village elders begged Deer Hunter to let her go. He ignored them, and an air of grim expectancy settled over the village.

The couple returned to their home, but before many days had passed, Deer

Hunter noticed that his wife was beginning to have an unpleasant odor. Then he saw that her beautiful face had grown ashen and her skin dry. At first he only turned his back on her as they slept. Later he began to sit up on the roof all night, but White Corn Maiden always joined him. In time the villagers became used to the sight of Deer Hunter racing among the houses and through the fields with White Corn Maiden, now not much more than skin and bones, in hot pursuit.

Things continued in this way, until one misty morning a tall and imposing figure appeared in the small dance court at the center of the village. He was dressed in spotless white buckskin robes and carried the biggest bow anyone had ever seen. On his back was slung a great quiver with the two largest arrows anyone had ever seen. He remained standing at the center of the village and called, in a voice that carried into every home, for Deer Hunter and White Corn Maiden. Such was its authority that the couple stepped forward meekly and stood facing him.

The awe–inspiring figure told the couple that he had been sent from the spirit

Three dancers
Oqwa Pi

world because they, Deer Hunter and White Corn Maiden, had violated their people's traditions and angered the spirits; that because they had been so selfish, they had brought grief and near–disaster to the village. "Since you insist on being together," he said, "you shall have your wish. You will chase one another forever across the sky, as visible reminders that your people must live according to tradition if they are to survive." With this he set Deer Hunter on one arrow and shot him low into the western sky. Putting White Corn Maiden on the other arrow, he placed her just behind her husband.

That evening the villagers saw two new stars in the west. The first, large and very bright, began to move east across the heavens. The second, a smaller, flickering star, followed close behind. So it is to this day, according to the Tewa; the brighter one is Deer Hunter, placed there in the prime of his life. The dimmer star is White Corn Maiden, set there after she had died; yet she will forever chase her husband across the heavens.

Tewa tale, translated by Alfonso Ortiz

THE SPHYNX MOTH AND THE OLD COYOTE

There once lived at Picurís Pueblo a Sphynx Moth and his grandmother. The Sphynx Moth was a great believer; he believed everything concerning the customs of the people. And he was very obedient to his grandmother; he would go wherever his grandmother would tell him, without talking back.

Once his grandmother said to him: "My grandson, you must make plumeros [Spanish: feather bunches] to-night and take them to Kan'in'ai ["At the Buffalo Track"], to the southeast, early to-morrow morning. The Picurís youths and even Picurís maidens take their plumeros there and supplicate. So early tomorrow morning you must carry these plumeros and go there to supplicate." So that night the Sphynx Moth made plumeros the way his grandmother had told him.

Early the next morning, carrying the plumeros, he set out for Kan'in'ai, to the southeast. As he went along through the fields, he met Old Coyote, who was hunting around. "Good morning, where are you going?" the Old Coyote said to the Sphynx Moth. "I am going over southeast to Kan'in'ai," said the Sphynx Moth. "What is it that you are carrying?" said the Old Coyote to the Sphynx Moth. Then the Sphynx Moth said: "I am carrying my dead grandmother over southeast to Kan'in'ai." Then the Old Coyote said: "Then wait here for me, for I am going to get my grandmother."

As Old Coyote told the Sphynx Moth thus, he ran toward Tciuthotha ["Eagle Pile Mountain"] where his own grandmother was. When he arrived there he hunted for a bag and went inside the house where his grandmother was toasting corn meal. And he said to his grandmother: "Grandmother, get into this bag!" But the grandmother would not get into it. "Get in here, I tell you," said Old Coyote to his grandmother. But his grandmother would not get in. The Old Coyote said: "If you do not get in, I will hit you on the head with a fire poker and then put you in this bag." The Old Coyote told his grandmother thus several times, but he soon got disgusted and, taking the fire poker which was lying by the fireplace, he struck his grandmother, where she was sitting toasting the corn meal, and then putting her into the bag and carrying her, he brought his grandmother over to where the Sphynx Moth was waiting for him. "Now we shall both take our grandmothers over southeast to Kan'in'ai," said the Old Coyote to the Sphynx Moth. The Sphynx Moth assented.

Then they both started off to Kan'in'ai, to the southeast. As they went along talking on the road they reached Kan'in'ai. There in a rocky place the Sphynx Moth dug, and laid his plumeros. When the Old Coyote noticed what the Sphynx Moth was doing, he discovered that instead of a dead grandmother it was plumeros that he was laying under a rock. And the Old Coyote said to himself: "This Sphynx Moth has told me a lie. Instead of having a dead grandmother in his bag, he is putting the plumeros under the rock. Now, I will go over there where he is and bite him." As the Sphynx Moth heard him saying thus, he flew away. Then the Old Coyote was very angry, and he said to himself: "That accursed Sphynx Moth, it is on account of him that I have killed my grandmother." As the Sphynx Moth disappeared as soon as he flew, the Old Coyote did not know what to do. Again he packed his grandmother on his back, and started for home. He was crying as he went along the road.

As he reached home, his children heard him crying from where they were playing, and said to each other: "But why is it that our father is so happy? He is coming along the road singing. Let us all go to meet him." As they said thus, the little Coyotes went to meet their father. When they met him, they asked him: "Our father, why are you so happy? Why are you coming along singing so loud?" Then their father told them: "My children, I am not coming along singing, but I am coming along crying. It is on account of that accursed Sphynx Moth that I have killed my grandmother by hitting her on the head, because he told me a lie. If I had known this, I would have bitten him while I had a chance." As their father told the little Coyotes thus, they all joined crying. The Old Coyote carried his grandmother into the house and set her down again at the fireplace where she had sat toasting corn meal, and gave her the corn meal toasting sticks and told her, although she was dead: "Now, grandmother, finish toasting your corn meal!" As he would set her down she would topple over again, and at last the Old Coyote got more angry, and he took the fire poker and struck his grandmother again on the head, to be sure that she had been killed. Then he put her on his back and took her to the arroyo to bury her.

So this is the reason that coyotes nowadays are smart, because they learned this kind of work long ago; this is the reason that the coyotes are smarter than any other four-footed animal.

You have a tail.

Picuris tale, retold by John P. Harrington

THE WATERMELON RACE

There is nothing the People like better than to have foot races. This may be because in the long ago, the gods of the People always settled their problems by means of foot races.

One day, very soon after the Indians had reached Keatwah, a place to the north, the twin gods Moyachuntanah, the Great Star, and Mokwanosenah, the Morning Star, made a journey to this village and, calling the chiefs of the pueblo, said to them: "Call your people, and let them take part in foot races. We have not had one for a long time."

The chiefs did as the gods asked them. All day long the people came to the appointed place. They came from the East, from the West, from the North, and from the South.

Watermelon Break (1978)
Helen Hardin

When all had gathered, Mokwanosenah asked, "Have all arrived?"

"Yes," answered one of the chiefs. "Even the children are here."

"Very well," said the Morning Star. "I am bringing a new fruit to the Pueblo People. Not one of you has ever tasted it. The first to taste it will be the winner of the race which we are about to begin. It will be the prize. From its seed will spring many more of its kind, so that all of you will enjoy it in due time. Now choose two runners, a young boy and a young girl, and let the race begin."

The Pueblo People did as they were told, all anxious to see who would win the race and almost certain that the young man would be the winner. It has always been known that a man is much stronger than a woman in foot races, although there are some girls who run as well as men.

All preparations having been made for the race, the watermelon, the prize fruit, was placed at the race goal. The signal was given and the runners were off.

They seemed like little birds fluttering through the air, they ran so fast. But, although the young girl was very swift running, she could not catch up with the young man. He sped like an arrow, soon reached the goal, and grasping the watermelon, held it above his head, showing the spectators that he had won the race.

And how do you suppose the young girl felt? Well, it is said that she was very disappointed and sad. The Great Star, who was always kind and ready to cheer his people and make them happy, saw how sad she was and said to her, "Do not be sad, little one, I shall give you a prize also. From today on, girls will always be more beautiful than boys, and the man will usually be stronger than the woman."

Upon hearing this, the young girl went off by herself to rest and came to the bank of a little stream. She was very tired after her race. No one noticed her absence, because they were looking and wondering at the unexpected new fruit, the watermelon.

Having rested a while on the silky soft grass, the young girl started to get up and saw herself in the water of the river. She was so pleased at what she saw that she forgot she had lost the race and went back to rejoin her friends.

From that day to this, the words of Moyachuntanah have come true. Girls, as a rule, are prettier than boys, although boys are stronger.

Carmen Gertrudis Espinosa

THE DELIGHT MAKERS

The old man gave a friendly nod to his grandchild, and crossed the threshold, stooping low. Still lower the tall form had to bend while entering the kitchen door. He announced his coming to the inmate in a husky voice and the common formula—

"Guatzena!"

"Raua,—'good,'" the woman replied.

Her father squatted close to the fire and fixed his gaze on his daughter. She knelt on the floor busy spreading dough or thick batter on a heated slab over the fire. She was baking corn-cakes,—the well-known *tortillas* as they are called to-day.

After a short pause the old man quietly inquired,—

"My child, where is your husband?"

"Zashue Tihua," the woman answered, without looking up or interrupting her work, "is in the fields."

"When will he come?"

The woman raised her right hand, and pointed to the hole in the wall, whence light came in from the outside. The wall faced the west, and the height of the loop–hole corresponded to that of the sun about one hour before sunset.

"Give food to the children," directed the old man. "When they have eaten and are gone I shall speak to you."

The fire crackled and blazed, and ruddy flashes shot across the features of the woman. Was it a mere reflection of the fire, or had her features quivered and colored? The old man scanned those features with a cold, steady look.

She removed from the fire the sooty pot of clay in which venison cut in small pieces was stewing together with corn, dark beans, and a few roots and herbs as seasoning. Then she called out,—

"Shyuote, come and eat! Where is Okoya?"

The latter alone heard the invitation, for Shyuote had gone to sleep on the hides. The elder brother shook him, and went into the kitchen. He was followed by the child who staggered from drowsiness. The mother meanwhile had placed on the floor a pile of corn-cakes. Beside it, in an earthen bowl decorated inside and out with geometrical lines, steamed the stew. Dinner was ready, the table spread.

To enjoy this meal both lads squatted, but Shyuote, still half asleep, lost his balance and tumbled over. Angry at the merriment which this created, the boy hastily grabbed the food, but his mother interfered.

"Don't be so greedy, uak,—'urchin.' Remember Those Above," she said; and Shyuote, imitating the example of Okoya, crossly muttered a prayer, and scattered crumbs before him. Then only, both fell to eating.

This was done by simply folding a slice of the cake to form a primitive ladle, and dipping the contents of the stew out with it. Thus they swallowed meat, broth, and finally the ladle also. Okoya arose first, uttering a plainly audible hoa. Shyuote ate longer; at last he wiped his mouth with the seam of his wrap, grumbled something intended for thanksgiving, and strolled back to his resting place in the front room. Okoya went out into the court-yard to be alone with his forebodings. The sight of his mother seemed oppressive to him.

After the boys had gone the woman emptied the remainder of the stew back

Woman Making Piki Bread
R. Joesyesva

into the pot, filled the painted bowl with water, and put both vessels in a corner. Then she sat down, leaning against the wall, looking directly toward her father. Her face was thin and wan, her cheeks were hollow, and her eyes had a suppressed look of uneasiness.

The old man remained quietly indifferent as long as the meal lasted; then he rose, peeped cautiously into the outer apartment, resumed his seat, and spoke in a low tone—

"Is it true that you have listened to kamonyitza, 'black corn'?"

The woman started. "Who says so?" she answered with sudden haste.

"The Koshare," replied the old man, looking at her with a cold steady gaze.

"What do I care for them," exclaimed his daughter. Her lips curled with an air of disdain.

"It may be," spoke her father, in measured tones, "that you do not wish to hear from them; but I know that they care for your doings."

"Let them do as they please."

"Woman," he warned, "speak not thus. Their disposition toward you is not a matter for indifference."

"What reason have they to follow my path? I am a woman like many others in the tribe, nothing more or less. I stay with my husband," she went on with greater animation, "I do my duty. What have the Delight Makers to say that might not be for my good?"

"And yet, you are not precious to them—"

"Neither are they precious to me," she cried. Her eyes sparkled.

Her father heaved a deep sigh. He shook his head and said in a husky tone—

"Woman, your ways are wrong. I know it, and the Koshare know it also. They may know more, much more than I could wish," he added, and looked into her eyes with a searching sorrowful glance. An awful suspicion lay in this penetrating look. Her face flushed, she bent her head to avoid his gaze.

To the gloomy talk succeeded a still more gloomy silence. Then the woman lifted her head, and began entreatingly—

"My father, I do not ask you to tell me how you come to know all this; but tell me, umo, what are these Delight Makers, the Koshare? At every dance they appear and always make merry. The people feel glad when they see them. They must be very wise. They know of everything going on, and drag it before people

Prayer for Rain (1981)
Marcellus Medina

to excite their mirth at the expense of others. How is it that they know so much? I am but a woman, and the ways of the men are not mine," she raised her face and her eyes flamed; "but since I hear that the Delight Makers wish me no good, I want to know at least what those enemies of mine are."

The old man lowered his glance and sighed.

"My child," he began softly, "when I was young and a boy like your son Okoya, I cared little about the Koshare. Now I have learned more." He leaned his head against the wall, pressed his lips firmly together, and continued.

"The holders of the paths of our lives, those who can close them when the time comes for us to go to Shipapu, where there is neither sorrow nor pain, have many agents among us. Pāyatyama our Father, and Sanashtyaya our Mother saw that the world existed ere there was light, and so the tribe lived in the dark. Four are the wombs in which people grew up and lived, ere Maseua and Oyoyāuā his brother led them to where we are now, and this world which is round like a shield is the fourth womb."

The woman listened with childlike eagerness. Her parted lips and sparkling eyes testified that everything was new to her.

"Father," she interrupted, "I knew nothing of this. You are very wise. But why are women never told such things?"

"Don't cut off my speech," he said. "Because women are so forward, that is why many things are concealed from them."

Adolf F. Bandelier

ANTIDOTE FOR TOBACCO

White Oak Bark, pulverized.......................4 ounces.
Capsicum...4 Grains.
Moisten with gum arabic sufficient to make it stick together. A chew is about the size of a bean several times a day. In three or four days desire for tobacco will be gone. Whenever you want tobacco take a chew of the above preparation.

J. I. Lighthall

THE SNAKES OF TESUQUE, 1924

Once upon a time a handsome youth came into a house and asked a girl to be his lover. She consented, and he told her to keep him secreted in a large jar. She locked him in an unused room, but when she returned to visit him he was not to be found. Remembering his words, she peeped into a vessel and saw a large snake coiled there. In due time she gave birth to two snakes. Her father angrily reproved her, and took the snakes into the hills, released them, gave them meal, and begged them not to harm people.

It is in memory of this incident that the village of Tesuque keeps two snakes. All the pueblos used to do so. The present custodian of the snakes is Alario Vigilo. Formerly each cacique kept one of the snakes, but now they appoint a Pa nu-pufonu (snake shaman), or Pa nu-ke (snake strong), for this duty. He feeds them three times a day with meal, pollen, and feathers. They are asked to send rain, to remain in the mountains away from the village. We do not kill snakes. We give them meal and ask them to go into the mountains and not harm us. A man who is bitten by a snake goes at once to the Summer cacique, who knows how to cure him with herbs. He is kept in seclusion until he recovers. And he must not come in sight of fire, lest he die.

Edward S. Curtis

WITCHCRAFT

The wind of early spring creeping down from the high peaks above Santa Fe still contained enough of winter's chill so the motley assortment of Indians, Mexicans, and Anglo–Americans crowding the old plaza pulled serapes or buffalo hide coats tighter about their bodies. It was a March evening, 1854, less than a decade after the United States had seized the Southwest from Mexico, and the New Mexico Territorial Court was in session. In a room dimly lit by candles, within the mud walls of the venerable Governor's Palace, the Honorable Grafton Baker, Chief Justice, presided. Not everyone in the curious throng had been able to find a place in the tightly packed courtroom, and the overflow had spilled into the adobe square outside. The case under consideration and exciting such interest was that of four Nambé Indians, accused of executing two of their fellow tribesmen for witchcraft.

According to the story pieced together from numerous accusations, the two murdered men, Luís Romero and Antonio Tafolla, had been practicing witches who devoured children of their village, witnesses having seen them pull bones of the victims from their mouths and noses. A council of all the people had been called, evidence presented, and the death penalty pronounced. Thereupon the executioners were named and they went out of the pueblo at dusk with the two condemned men who were made to kneel side by side and were then felled by a single shotgun blast to the head.

Upon word of the incident, the new territorial authorities arrested the four Indians actually involved in the killing, although it was apparent the entire village was implicated. The matter had aroused some consternation among the native populace, both Indian and Spanish, because it could not be understood why anyone would object to the removal of dangerous witches from a community. The officers of Nambé, speaking through court interpreters, explained that having full jurisdiction to administer the internal affairs of the pueblo, they considered it their duty to search out evildoers and inflict appropriate punishment. That they had this authority was not challenged. The issue concerning the court was whether witchcraft actually existed and could be considered a crime under the law.

The most important person to testify was the Indian governor of Nambé, Juan Ignacio Tapolla, who unhesitatingly admitted that by common assent the two witches had been done away with in the manner described. Part of his testimony ran as follows:

The four defendants came and reported to me that they had killed Luis Romero and Antonio Tafolla, in accordance with the order of the pueblo. It was done in the beginning of this month. They only said they had killed them; I did not see them after they were killed. They were killed at twilight not quite a league from the pueblo, in a north direction. I saw them going out with the deceased; they had a shotgun. Juan Diego carried the gun. I saw them when they came back to report to me. They were killed by order of the pueblo and the head men of the pueblo. I am the governor of the pueblo, and Juan Diego is the fiscal ["constable"]. It was the duty of the fiscal to execute the orders of the pueblo. They commanded him to kill these two men. The bad acts spoken of were that they were detected in the act of witchcraft and sorcery: they had eaten up the little children of the pueblo. It has always been our custom to put a stop to and check bad acts. We have not exercised this custom of killing witches since the Americans came here, because there had not been such doings before. This act was done by the command of myself and the whole pueblo.

Torturing a Sorcerer
Farny

Marc Simmons

MAGPIE DROWNS BLUE CORN GIRL

Magpie and his wife, Blue Corn maiden, lived at the cottonwood. Blue Corn maiden was very playful and jolly. She liked to tease everybody, her ways and manner were full of fun. Magpie had an old humpback bow with which he was practicing and exercising to learn the sound of the bow string tied on the bow. He would beat the bow string with his arrow and study the sound—tew tew! Finally he was prepared. The first day he told his wife that he was going to go out on the hunt. He went and stayed in a hiding place to watch his wife coming out

Dressing Young Girl for First Ceremonial (1937)
Pablita Velarde (Tse Tsan), Santa Clara

from the house. The first day she went to the east to see and converse with the men she found. Magpie came home in the evening first. Then his wife came in late. Then Magpie got his bow out and held his bow close to his ear, beating his bow with an arrow. And his wife was listening. Every time he beat his bow, he said, "*Hah* (yes), *hugaihu* (and then)," making his wife believe that he talked with his bow, which was telling him of what his wife was doing during the day when she was out on the east side of the house. The second day Magpie started on the hunt, but he stayed again at his hiding place. His wife came out from the house and started to the north side. She did the same thing as the first day, she talked to a man. Magpie came in the evening, got his bow and beat the same as before, striking with the arrow on the string and making the same reply as before—"Yes, and then." The third day Magpie started again on the hunt, again he stayed at his hiding place. His wife came out again from the house and started to the west. She did the same thing as before, she talked to a man. Magpie came in the evening, got his bow and beat the same as before, striking with the arrow on the bow, striking the same reply as before—"Yes, and then." The fourth day Magpie started again on the hunt, he stayed at his hiding place. His wife came out again from the house, and started to the south. She did the same thing as before, she talked to a man. Magpie came in the evening, got his bow and beat the same as before, striking with the arrow on the bow. The string gave the same reply as before— "Yes, and then." After seeing all he saw about his wife, he put her under water to end her life.

Taos tale, retold by Elsie Clews Parsons

TRUE WAY OF THE SCALP DANCE

When our village came to being, the times were hard as the land was yet untamed. The people knew the ways of their ancestors and practiced them, going about the rituals without hesitating or relying upon others.

Such was the ritual of the Scalp Dance. A man knew within himself of his capabilities, his purposes and obligations; without so much as a word the man would set a time in his mind and proceed to execute what he made up his mind to do. He would go out alone, prepared for his undertaking, whether it would be right away or sometime in the future. So we were brought up with this knowledge and in my younger days when I participated in many rituals, I knew by instinct when a scalping would take place and what would follow. But the rituals would be kept in secrecy, especially when the Ahauda were involved, for they were a law unto the rituals.

Chants and prayers were the ways in which we expressed our feelings. Although the Ahauda were the most sacred in this particular ritual, and the most feared for their destructive ways because scalping was of their commands, the Ahauda were dear.

When a scalp was being brought into the village, the people awakened early in the morning and blessed themselves with the spirits of the dead brought to them by the breezes. Shortly, the procession was headed, led there by female relatives of the priests-to-be, to circle the village slaughtering horses, dogs, and other strays. However, it seems the people today who take part in these rituals deliberately delay the proceedings, therefore prolonging and in the process eliminating certain phases of the rituals.

The Ant Clan, the Batdonneh, and the Bow Priests who had such a ritual long ago, revealed to us that they had forgotten some details of the ceremonies. That seems incredible because from generation to generation our forefathers, no matter how much the length of time that passed between such rituals, whether one year or five years, never failed to display an event, showing such negligence. As many times as the Scalp Dance has been repeated, what causes the sudden lapse into forgetfulness?

A short time ago, when the ritual was once more partaken, each one of the priests-to-be balked and hesitated so ~~as to~~ delay for such a length of time that it was considered totally alien to the old ways. While in the days long ago, though problems at that time seemed impossible, the rituals were always carried on without a moment's delay and the dances were completed.

Our young people tend to take their time in doing anything today: then it was supposed that if a ritual was done in only the length of time necessary, the blessings given us would have the power of youth and vigor everlasting.

The Scalp Dance that took place not long ago neglected a number of important aspects of the ritual, such as the feather of the roadrunner worn by the initiates. Though I do not know exactly why the feather is important, I was told only a few words of its being. It is known that for some reason the Ant Clan saved the Ahauda when the brothers were asked to guess at what the roadrunner had done, whether it entered a small burrow or whether the tracks were leading away from the burrow. The older of the Ahauda was asked first for his answer, and he answered that the road-runner had gone out of the burrow, while his little brother answered that the roadrunner had gone in. There they were instructed to do what was going to be and then taken into the Knife Society. There the younger of the two was initiated into the Kachina cult, and the other only blessed so he would have the strength and courage for endurance and tolerance.

Because this happened, the Ant Clan members became their parents, so that when the Ahauda were prepared they were dressed the way they are, and the chants, prayers, and songs sung to them are theirs alone.

But again, because of the delay in the ceremonies today, the last time

Koshare (circa 1962)
Rose M. Gachupin

this happened the sons were not completed while the ritual of painting the Bow Priests was being done. As each garment is adorned upon them, prayers are said and chanted and songs sung. Until this has been done, the Bow Priests do not come after the scalps, but again, because of their negligence, these rituals have been somewhat altered. That on the morning, the last morning when the completion of the rituals takes place, each head of each ritual is to be adorned with the feathers that depict the greatness of natural elements.

For some time these rituals, even some social ceremonies, were almost abolished by the influence of the Spaniards, but as the ceremonies once more began to take place, the old people like me began to function as the leaders of the societies. And because we have kept our knowledge and preserved our ways, we have been kept in our posts of leadership, for rarely does a young person wish the knowledge we have to himself. One does not learn by keeping silent for I too had to inquire of many persons, some who no longer are among us, people like Hoonki who had learned from his father the true forms of expressing what we believed in.

Some of us remember what we have been told, especially about these rituals, wonder why it is we have intermingled with those who were considered our enemies. For now, our young people have intermingled with members of tribes we once warred against. These situations were feared and condemned many years ago and now we wonder if time has changed the way of the spirits, for we have been shown what could and might have happened. The blessings that we ask for ourselves are shown throughout the last phase of the ceremony when we offer arrows three times and the last when we give an offering of material value. These have come to being as they are now only through the efforts of a few who truly believe in the old ways and the spirits of our ancestors.

The Zuni people, translated by Alvina Quam

PART EIGHT

TWO WORLDS

SAN GERONIMO

"Come. Let us get up and do our work so we can see this fiesta. There is one thing about it I am going to like!"

How he hated it, this deer he had killed and which now struck him through his false security. For like all men he could endure the blows of adversity but not arrows which pricked his pride and vanity. And like most he blamed the invisible marksman rather than his own vulnerability.

The late afternoon, the pueblo and the pole drew them all. Apaches had come like buzzards to a kill—both those known as the Llaneros and the Olleros. Big dark men wearing great black Stetsons and silver ear-rings, and women bulging in pink and purple waists and striped petticoats. Pottery makers from the pueb–

Buffalo dancers
G. Casiquito

los down river had spread out on the ground their bowls and jars and little clay figures of skunk, deer, bear, rabbits and turtles. Some Uncompaghre Utes were down from the mountains; a lean Navajo had come from the desert with a load of silver and turquoise. Even a few Plains Indians, rich enough to come by train, stood beside Rena, their beautiful blankets draped carelessly over suits of wrinkled serge. They were talking sign-language with a tattered White River Ute—the expressive free-flowing gestures of dark, poetic hands that will always remain, unforgotten, the most expressive medium of their wordless souls. Everyone boasted his best clothes, his oldest buckskin. The sun gleamed on snowy boots and beaded moccasins, flowered shawls, silk shirts and colored blankets—all one vast blanket of color spread upon the plaza, and covering the terraced pueblo to the highest roof tops.

It had always stood between the lingering twilight of summer and the false dawn of fall which first begins to flame among the highest aspens. So they had danced the Sundown Dance after last evening's early Mass. Very beautifully, quietly, quickly, in all the wonder and the tremulous hush. A small group of old men filing out of the little church freshly whitewashed to reflect the pinkish glow of the setting sun. Standing in two lines, naked to the waist, in old buckskin leggings and new moccasins. Gently waving branches of green-leaved aspens left from summer, and the first branches of aspen leaves stained deep yellow, clear pink and spotted red. Singing softly, treading lightly, then quickly fading away into the dusk.

It had always marked the pendulum pause when the sun's summer race was over, and he began his winter journey. So early this morning the young men had raced down the long track in relays, toward San Geronimo watching from his shelter of green boughs at the finish.

For long too it had begun the great fall Fairs of a wilderness empire, and the plaza swarmed with travesties of lingering ghosts. Trappers in buckskin stepped out of long sleek automobiles. Mexican caballeros on spavined plow horses rode from La Oreja in skintight black trousers embroided in silver. Señoras in lace mantillas and high Spanish combs paraded, chewing gum and munching popcorn.

It was San Geronimo—an immemorial feast day whose roots were anchored deep in Indian earth, and whose branches held entwined the later traditions of

Mexican Fiesta and White Fair alike. But its trunk was still a tall, stripped pine pole planted in the plaza of the pueblo; and hanging down from the top a deer with its throat slashed open, corn and squash, and a dirty flour sack full of fresh bread and groceries.

There was a sudden whoop, a high-pitched yell. Howling and shrieking, six Indians dashed into the crowded plaza. All were naked but for breech clouts and moccasins, their faces and bodies smeared with black and white clay. They were the Black Eyes, the Koshares, the Chiffonetas—the fun-makers ever-present at most pueblo ceremonies. Really clowns, and very clever as they pranced around making horseplay, frightening children and pantomiming whites and Mexicans.

The Pueblo Indian is invariably patient and charitable to summer visitors. Yet in the antics of the Chiffonetas are revealed his acute perception and sly humor. One wears strapped to his arm a battered alarm clock. He looks at it. "It is time to be hungry!"—and he snatches from a bystander a bag of popcorn. Another owlishly puffs a pipe. Still an-

Koshares
Richard Martinez

other grabs a woman's hat for his own head, and as though on high heels minces off wiggling his naked hips. Civilization slapped on a savage who shows its ludicrous aspects.

But now their humor and pantomiming carried a touch of the malicious. The painted clowns strutted as tourists into doorways. They jerked open women's handbags to loudly demand in English of the contents, "How much this handkerchief? How much? This Indian?" Squatting on the ground, they drew a tiny square and bargained for it in lewd Spanish: This is Indian land. No good. We buy it for a drink of whiskey!" Two of the grotesque actors started off to the mountains to kill a deer. The other four set upon them, rolled them in the dust and gave them an imaginary beating. They were Government men, they shouted in their own tongue. And when the last one rose it was to snatch a kerchief from a spectator to wrap round his broken head, to spit upon it later and throw it down underfoot.

Most of the visitors sat forcing silly grins, knowing better than to resist and saving their cussing till later, or unaware of the meaning of the extravagant horseplay. But the Indians, seeing the ironic subtlety of the mimicry, smiled grimly at the howling, leaping figures.

Frank Waters

PUEBLO REALITY

You know how it is.

People come here and they want to know our secret of life.

They ask many questions but their minds are already made up.

They admire our children but they feel sorry for them.

They look around and they do not see anything except dust.

They come to our dances but they are always wanting to take pictures.

They come into our homes expecting to learn about us in five minutes.

Our homes, which are made of mud and straw, look strange to them.

They are glad they do not live here.

Yet they are not sure whether or not we know something which is the key to all
    understanding.

Our secret of life would take them forever to find out.

Even then, they would not believe it.

Anonymous Taos elder, retold by Nancy Wood

Marie and blond tourist
viewing pottery
Gilbert Atencio

KOPIS'TAYA (A GATHERING OF SPIRITS)

Because we live in the browning season
the heavy air blocking our breath,
and in this time when living
is only survival, we doubt the voices
that come shadowed on the air,
that weave within our brains
certain thoughts, a motion that is soft,
imperceptible, a twilight rain,
      soft feather's fall, a small body
dropping into its nest, rustling, murmuring,
settling in for the night.

Because we live in the hard-edged season,
where plastic brittle and gleaming shines
and in this space that is cornered and angled,
we do not notice wet, moist, the significant
drops falling in perfect spheres
that are the certain measures of our minds;
almost invisible, those tears,
soft as dew, fragile, that cling to leaves,
petals, roots, gentle and sure,
every morning.

We are the women of daylight; of clocks and steel
foundries, of drugstores and streetlights,
of superhighways that slice our days in two.

Wrapped around in glass and steel we ride
our lives; behind dark glasses we hide our eyes,
our thoughts, shaded, seem obscure, smoke
fills our minds, whisky husks our songs,
polyester cuts our bodies from our breath,
our feet from the welcoming stones of earth.
Our dreams are pale memories of themselves,
and nagging doubt is the false measure of our days.

Even so, the spirit voices are singing,
their thoughts are dancing in the dirty air.
Their feet touch the cement, the asphalt
delighting, still they weave dreams upon our
shadowed skulls, if we could listen.
If we could hear.
Let's go then. Let's find them. Let's
listen for the water, the careful gleaming drops
that glisten on the leaves, the flowers. Let's
ride the midnight, the early dawn. Feel the wind
striding through our hair. Let's dance
the dance of feathers, the dance of birds.

Paula Gunn Allen
Laguna/Sioux

PECOS WARRIORS AT JEMEZ

The Eagle Watchers Society was the sixth to go into the kiva at the summer and autumn rain retreats. It was an important society, and it stood apart from the others in a certain way. This difference—this superiority—had come about a long time ago. Before the middle of the last century, there was received into the population of the town a small group of immigrants from the Tanoan city of Bahkyula, a distance of seventy or eighty miles to the east. These immigrants were a wretched people, for they had experienced great suffering. Their land bordered upon the Southern Plains, and for many years they had been an easy mark for marauding bands of buffalo hunters and thieves. They had endured every kind of persecution until one day they could stand no more and their spirit broke. They gave themselves up to despair and were then at the mercy of the first alien wind. But it was not a human enemy that overcame them at last; it was a plague. They were struck down by so deadly a disease that when the epidemic abated, there were fewer than twenty survivors in all. And this remainder, too, should surely have perished among the ruins of Bahkyula had it not been for these *patrones*, these distant relatives who took them in at the certain risk of their own lives and the lives of their children and grandchildren. It is said that the cacique himself went out to welcome and escort the visitors in. The people of the town must have looked narrowly at those stricken souls who walked slowly toward them, wild in their eyes with grief and desperation. The Bahkyush immigrants brought with them little more than the clothes on their backs, but even in this moment of deep hurt and humiliation they thought of themselves as a people. They carried four things that should serve thereafter to signal who they were: a sacred flute; the bull and the horse masks of Pecos; and the little wooden statue of their patroness María de los Angeles, whom they called Porcingula. Now, after intervening years and generations, the ancient blood of this forgotten tribe still ran in the veins of men.

The Eagle Watcher Society was the principal ceremonial organization of the Bahkyush. Its chief, Patiestwa, and all its members were direct descendants of those old men and women who had made that journey along the edge of oblivion. There was a look about these men, even now. It was as if, conscious of having come so close to extinction, they had got a keener sense of humility than their benefactors, and paradoxically a greater sense of pride. Both attributes could be seen in such a man as old Patiestwa. He was hard, and he appeared to have seen more of life than had other men. In their uttermost peril long ago, the Bahkyush had been fashioned into seers and soothsayers. They had acquired a tragic sense, which gave to them as a race so much dignity and bearing. They were medicine men; they were rainmakers and eagle hunters.

N. Scott Momaday
Kiowa

THE PUEBLO INDIANS

The Pueblos believe that the Great One is omnipresent. They ask for permission to use the physical form of an animal before it is killed. They believe that animals have an inner spiritual component. This is the spiritual life they invoke with a short prayer. It is not a new idea; other natives throughout the Americas have this ritual. In taking branches from the sacred Douglas fir tree, the Pueblo men will inform the Creator that the intent is not to mutilate the tree, but that it will be used to decorate the human being in the performance of a sacred ritual or dance in His honor. In Pueblo religion, the Douglas fir is used to adorn most dancers, male and female. It is also used to decorate the altar and shrine, where a likeness of a patron saint is kept during the day of the feast. For many years Pueblo families did not have Christmas trees, since the purposes were not native. The dominant society often uses fir trees for Christmas trees. An unsold fir on a sales lot is a sad sight indeed, and is considered sacrilegious. This tree is not used to decorate a front yard either, since tradition has it that one is changing nature when a fir tree is dug up and moved to the yard in a Pueblo or a village.

Joe S. Sando
Jemez

HE IS NOT ONE OF US

When I was about thirteen years old I went down to St. Michael's Catholic School. Other boys were joining the societies and spending their time in the kivas being purified and learning the secrets. But I wanted to learn the white man's secrets. I thought he had better magic than the Indian. . . . So I drifted a little away from the pueblo life. My father was sad but he was not angry. He wanted me to be a good Indian like all the other boys, but he was willing for me to go to school. He thought I would soon stop. There was plenty of time to go into the kiva.

Then at the first snow one winter . . . a white man—what you call an Indian Agent—came and took all of us who were in that school far off on a train to a new kind of village called Carlisle Indian School, and I stayed there seven years. . . .

Seven years I was there. I set little letters together in the printing shop and we printed papers. For the rest we had lessons. There were games, but I was too slight for foot and hand plays, and there were no horses to ride. I learned to talk English and to read. There was much arithmetic. It was lessons: how to add and take away, and much strange business like you have crossword puzzles only with numbers. The teachers were very solemn and made a great fuss if we did not get the puzzles right.

There was something called Greatest Common Denominator. I remember the name but I never knew it—what it meant. When the teachers asked me I would guess, but I always guessed wrong. We studied little things—fractions. I remember that word too. It is like one half of an apple. And there were immoral fractions. . . .

They told us that Indian ways were bad. They said we must get civilized. I remember that word too. It means "be like the white man." I am willing to be like the white man, but I did not believe Indian ways were wrong. But they kept teaching us for seven years. And the books told how bad the Indians had been to white men—burning their towns and killing their women and children. But I had seen the white men do that to Indians. We all wore white man's clothes and ate white man's food and went to white man's churches and spoke white man's talk. And so after a while we also began to say Indians were bad. We laughed at our own people and their blankets and cooking pots and sacred societies and dances. I tried to learn the lessons—and after seven years I came home. . . .

It was a warm summer evening when I got off the train at Taos station. The first Indian I met, I asked him to run out to the pueblo and tell my family I was home. The Indian couldn't speak English. And I had forgotten all my Pueblo language. But after a while he learned what I meant and started running to tell my father "Tulto is back. . . . "

We chattered and cried, and I began to remember many Indian words, and they told me about an uncle, Tha–a–ba, who had just died, and how Turkano, my old friend, had finished his year's fast and was joining the Black–eyes to become a priest and delight–maker.

Two little sisters and many little cousins had come along with the family to meet me. All these children liked me and kept running up and feeling my white man's clothes and then running away laughing. The children tried to repeat the English words I said, and everyone was busy teaching me Pueblo words again. We sat down on the grass and talked until it became very dark. . . .

I went home with my family. And the next morning the governor of the pueblo and the two war chiefs and many of the priest chiefs came into my father's house. They did not talk to me; they did not even look at me. When they were all assembled they talked to my father.

The chiefs said to my father, "Your son who calls himself Rafael has lived with the white men. He has been far away from the pueblo. He has not lived in the kiva nor learned the things that Indian boys should learn. He has no hair. He has no blankets. He cannot even speak our language and he has a strange smell. He is not one of us."

The chiefs got up and walked out. My father was very sad. I wanted him to be angry, but he was only sad. So I would not be sad and was very angry instead.

And I walked out of my father's house and out of the pueblo. I did not speak. My mother was in the other room cooking. She stayed in the other room but she made much noise rattling her pots. Some children were on the plaza and they stared at me, keeping very still as I walked away.

I walked until I came to the white man's town, Fernandez de Taos. I found work setting type in a printing shop there. Later I went to Durango and other towns in Wyoming and Colorado, printing and making a good living. But this indoor work was bad for me. It made me.slight of health. So then I went outside to the fields. I worked in blacksmith shops and on farms.

All this time I was a white man. I wore white man's clothes and kept my hair cut. I was not very happy. I made money and I kept a little of it and after many years I came back to Taos.

My father gave me some land from the pueblo fields. He could do this because now the land did not belong to all the people, as it did in the old days; the white man had cut it up and given it in little pieces to each family, so my father gave me part of his, and I took my money and bought some more land and some cattle. I built a house just outside the pueblo. I would not live in the pueblo so I built a house bigger than the pueblo houses all for myself.

My father brought me a girl to marry. Her name was Roberta. Her Indian name was P'ah–tah–zhuli (little deer bean). She was about fifteen years old and she had no father. But she was a good girl and she came to live with me in my new house outside the pueblo.

When we were married I became an Indian again. I let my hair grow, I put on blankets, and I cut the seat out of my pants.

Sun Elk
Taos

Female Harvest Corn Dance (1960)
Gilbert Atencio

MY GREAT-GRANDMOTHER

My great-grandmother was Maria Anaya
from Paguate village north of Old Laguna.
She had married my great-grandfather, Robert G.
   Marmon,
after her sister, who had been married to him,
died. There were two small children then,
and she married him so the children would have
   a mother.
She had been sent East
to the Indian school at Carlisle
and she later made a trip
with the children to Ohio
where my great-grandpa's relatives, the Marmons,
   lived
My great-grandpa didn't go with them and
he never seemed much interested in returning to
   Ohio.
He had learned to speak Laguna
and Grandpa Hank said when great-grandpa
   went away from Laguna
white people who knew
sometimes called him "Squaw Man."
Grandpa Hank and his brother Kenneth
were just little boys

when my great-grandfather took them
on one of his trips to Albuquerque.
The boys got hungry
so great-grandpa started to take them
through the lobby of the only hotel in
   Albuquerque
at that time.
Grandpa Hank said that when the hotel manager
spotted him and Kenneth
the manager stopped them
He told Grandpa Marmon that he was always
   welcome.
when he was alone
but when he had Indians with him
he should use the back entrance to reach the café.
My great-grandfather said,
"These are my sons."
He walked out of the hotel
and never would set foot in that hotel again
not even years later
when they began to allow Indians inside.

Leslie Marmon Silko
Laguna

TOWA

Before communities of strangers settled,
marking Pueblo boundaries
and changing the arid
open landscape forever,
there were people of Black Mesa,
who called themselves Towa.
People whose clear, brown eyes witnessed
Star explosions high above them,
against a celestial canvas of darkness.
The Towa were filled with mystery,
wonder
and reverence
for the universe encircling them.
Reverence gave birth to ritual,
celebration wove ceremony
into songs that blanketed the village
with life-giving spirit.
Planting nourishment for the children of Puye,
with steady handwork,
bedding seeds of corn,
squash
and beans.
Drum beats pounded upward,
introducing a new season's fertile ground.
Nimble fingers pressing seedlings into earth
    beds,
Digging,
planting,
covering and smoothing
in perpetual motion,

connecting each Towa
to the cycle of plant life.
From the heavens, to the rain-drenched earth
    beds,
to the seedlings ripened into colored corn.
From the harvest to the Corn Dance.
Clay-skinned people,
danced with willowlike movements,
then melted quietly into waiting earth beds.
Seedlings creating another
and yet another of these Towa.
The plant and human life cycle,
equal in symmetry.
This was before change disrupted night's mystery
and other world views crowded into Pueblo
    boundaries.
Now Towa rush to their jobs outside of village
    walls,
adapting to standards unlike their own.
Dressing our clay-skinned bodies
in image conscious fashion,
we stroke this new life of comfort.
Yet, somewhere in us,
persistent sounds surge upward
reminding us of our life cycles,
and the innocent wonder
that is our birthright,
as children of Towa.

Nora Naranjo-Morse
Santa Clara

ECHO FROM BEYOND

We are the First Inhabitants
Of Jemez Pueblo.
We are the ones
Who traveled South
From the mountains,
With bows in hand,
In the prime
Of our youth.

It was we who
Broke the trails
To your hunting grounds,
Cleared the land
Which is your lifeline,
Harnessed the river
Which waters your fields,
We, who with wet–
streaked faces,
Saw in
Setting sun the
Promise of Tomorrow.

Here we lived
And loved,
Fought and drove the Spaniards,
The Apaches, the Navajos,
And the Comanches,
From our fields
And homes.
Built the kivas
For your recreation

And education.
We served our turn.
We laid the
Strong foundations.
We are content.
Look not back
Too long
Too often
But build, like us,
Carry on,
For your sons,
For a better day
Tomorrow.

Joe S. Sando
Jemez

Zia Pueblo Potter
Velino Shije Herrera

MIXED BLOOD

Venustiano De Vargas came honestly by his name through his father, one of whose father's fathers had been horse–boy to the original De Vargas of the Conquistadores, and on his mother's side he was, as a member of the Calabasa Clan, entitled to land and office in the northernmost of the Rio Grande pueblos [Taos]. That he was a man grown and the father of a family before the latter of these honors came to him was owing to his having become, in the meantime, a Presbyterian. It had happened to him at Indian Board[ing] School, where, in the interval after his father had been killed in a drunken brawl, and before she had married Albert Looking Elk, his mother had been glad to place him. There, being of a religious temperament and having no occasion for instruction in his own tribal rites, he fell under the influence of missionaries, believed the prayers and sang the hymns with great gusto, and, with all his Indian blood, lacking other affiliations, was glad to call himself by their name.

At the end of eight years of Board[ing] School, Venustiano got himself a job on the railroad, made the soundly Presbyterian gesture of refusing to let his hair grow, and on his occasional visits to his mother reminded her that he was of mixed blood and no Indian. This was a situation to which nobody paid any attention until he fell in love with Abieta of the Turquoise Clan, and, reminding himself that if he was of mixed blood he might as well have advantage of it, asked for an allotment of pueblo land and moved into the two rooms that Abieta built for him next to her mother's. In the beginning Venustiano rather sported his alien strain, kept his hair short, refused to eat jack–rabbit for four days in preparation for the Race of the Swift–Coming Rain, and, when the young men came up out of the kiva blowing eagle down for lightness, he was not among them. Also he went to his communal work in the simple nakedness of pants, without a blanket, and found that he was put out by caustic comments of the other men and the reprimands of the Cacique. But the Cacique was old and blind, so that nothing much came of it until, after three years, the Cacique died, and his successor turned out to be Venustiano's material uncle, who took it as an affront that one of the family should go about refusing the tribal rites because he was a Presbyterian. There were plenty of men in the pueblo who did not let the circumstance of their being good Catholics interfere with their coming to the communal work properly swathed as to their legs and with their hair falling forward over their shoulders in two long tails appropriately wound with the strips of beaver. Nor did making the Roman sign inhibit the salutatory pinch of sacred meal on entering a friend's house, nor blowing down for lightness in preparation for the ceremonial races. Since nothing in pueblo custom inhibited the utilization of as many rites as a man found served his purpose, it was distinctly a matter of bad form for Venustiano to assume so much on the mere ground of being a Presbyterian.

The Cacique called a Council of the Elders to remonstrate with the representative of mixed blood, at which much was said, with gravity and emotion, about being faithful to the beliefs of the fathers and the time-honored custom.

"Me," said Venustiano, speaking in English which seemed somehow to have become a point of doctrine, "I don't make nothing with those old gods. I get me a God that is the true one and not no old people's story. I got me a religion that's got nothing to do with clothes and letting your hair grow, an' I'm gonna keep it."

"Then," said the Cacique, at the point of tears, "never call me uncle again."

"Well," said Venustiano, not far from tears himself and not admitting it, "I don't know if I want to call any old fool like you uncle." Whereat the Elders put their hands over their mouths with astonishment, and the Governor, as soon as he could articulate, responded with a leaf out of Venustiano's English book. "I fine you fifteen dollars for contempt of court," he said, which Venustiano could not but feel was taking an excess of advantage.

After that, when he arrived for his turn at cleaning the communal ditch, the Cacique ordered him off until he could make up his mind to appear in pueblo dress. Three days later, the Elders unhooked his team which he had harnessed to plough the widow's field, and Venustiano suffered in his most Indian feelings which yearned toward the communal obligation as a prideful necessity. It wasn't, as he complained to his wife and his wife's mother

CLAY

[Clay], that stuff of the earth, which we work with, talk with, identify with, and create with. It is so much a part of us that the same Tewa word, "nung," is used for both earth (clay) and us (people). I have a daughter who is a clay person out of whom other clay people emerge.

Rina Swentzell
Santa Clara

Looking East
**Kimberly Sisneros,
age 11, Tewa**

and Albert Looking Elk, that he cared what the Cacique or the Elders said to him, but that they ought to remember that he was after all of mixed blood and proper Indian feelings. In June, they refused to enumerate his two infant children in the school census, and that summer he heard his wife crying in the night because, she said, the women who went to wash at the creek took up their bundles and moved away when she tried to wash beside them. That fall she gathered plums alone by the creek borders and braided her strings of six-colored corn un-aided.

In September, on the Saint's day, which was also the day of the ceremonial races, Venustiano, to make up for not being invited to any of the festal parties, bought himself a pair of store-new ready-made pants with a lavender stripe in them, and Abieta admitted to her maternal aunt that she couldn't see why, when there were so many conformable religions, her husband should have chosen the most unconformable. This aunt, Tsinina, was a woman of great character who had married a Jicarilla Apache, with whom on feast-days she returned regularly to the pueblo. She was a wise woman, wise in tribal ways, with the power of dreaming true, and great kindliness of spirit. Husbands, she said, who gave themselves to strange religions could not be argued with, but they might be managed. Plainly, Presbyterianism was a kind of *brujería* against which any wife was justified in creating an opportunity. She might even set up a counter-*brujería*, as, for instance, since pants were Venustiano's obsession, against that, a figure of him stripped of his proud bifurcated possession, blanket encased, to hide with appropriate rites in the brush sheathing of the ceiling over his bed.

Nothing happened for a week or two, and then the *brujería* began to work. The pueblo's official interpreter went hunting on Monte Piedra, and, by the time he was completely out of call, the local Indian Agent arrived with the word that the head of Indian education was expected shortly to consummate the arrangement of adding two new grades to the village school. It was a matter of the utmost community concern, since the new arrangement would keep the boys at home past the time when they should be put to their kiva training, so that all the village was agog with it, and scouts were out to retrieve the missing interpreter. It was a matter of anxiety, because the only other possible candidate for that office was Venustiano, who had already once served at it. It was Aunt Tsinina who had word in a dream of the arrival of the educational head at the nearest white settlement, and the certainty that unless the interpreter turned up in the morning, as she felt sure he wouldn't, Venustiano must hold himself in readiness. She made a grave and tactful speech on the gratification it gave her to think of the husband of her favorite niece in a situation of such eminent service to his community, and Venustiano was much moved by it. "I rather fancy," he said to his wife, "I can do myself credit in that capacity," and went to bed especially early by way of preparation, before Aunt Tsinina had finished pottering around. In the morning, by the time the messenger commandeered for that purpose arrived from the Governor, who had held off to the last possible moment, Venustiano was clothed in his woolen drawers and his new pink and purple checked shirt, but ohé and alas! the time shortened, and nobody could so much as lay a finger on the new pants with the lavender stripes. They were not on the pole of the soft stuff, which was stripped to the search, and failed to be discovered under the bed, where they might have been expected, or in the tin trunk which was left over from his railroading days. Venustiano was as nearly excited as it is permitted even a mixed blood to be, and Aunt Tsinina in an excess of helpfulness undertook to clean the spots off his old blue overalls, with the result that they were rendered unusable by the condition of sopping wetness. "Oh well," said Tsinina, surveying the nearest male relatives who had gathered to the crisis, for it was rumored that a second, more urgent messenger was on his way from the Governor, "take this," appropriating what appeared to be the newest blanket, in magenta with cerise stripes. "The color does set you off something handsome," she allowed, proceeding to swathe Venustiano's lower limbs with it. With a hasty glance at himself in the ten-cent-store mirror, Venustiano came also to the opinion. He could tell by the way the Governor's face lightened, as he came into the presence, that he had scored. And in that certainty the interpreting went so well that by dinner-time he was able to forget, not only the misadventure of the missing pants, but to accept several cordial slaps on the back as a tribute to his linguistic powers, with no reference to his relenting from his recalcitrance in the matter of tribal dress. He spent his evening bargaining with the cousin for the cerise and magenta blanket, and turned up in it the third day when ground was ceremonially broken for the additional two rooms to the schoolhouse. Everyone was having a hand in it with a heartiness which so stirred the Indian blood of Venustiano that, when somebody handed him a shovel, he couldn't quite make up his mind to refuse it. What he waited for was the flick of the eyes that passed from the Governor to the Cacique, took in his blanketed lower limbs, and admitted him to the community of labor. Venustiano tucked up the ends of his blanket and shovelled manfully.

RELIGION

We have no word that translates what is meant by "religion." We have a spiritual life that is part of us twenty-four hours a day. It determines our relationship with the natural world and our fellow man. Our religious practices are the same as in the time of our ancestors.

Anonymous
Jemez State Monument

A week later, Aunt Tsinina went back to Jicarilla with her husband. "Do you know," she said to Abieta, "I've had a dream about those pants of Venustiano's. I think they are at the bottom of the wheat–bin under all that wheat. But I wouldn't dig them up again. I'd just let them come to light naturally. You can't always tell what these mixed bloods will think about things."

Mary Austin

Turkeys
Pablita Velarde

EASY LIFE OF THE GRAY-EYED

I can just remember the old men of my village. Old age was simply a delightful time, when the old men sat on the sunny doorsteps, playing in the sun with the children, until they fell asleep. At last they failed to wake up.

These old, old men used to prophesy about the coming of the white man. They would go about tapping with their canes on the adobe floor of the house, and call to us children:

"Listen! Listen! The gray-eyed people are coming nearer and nearer. They are building an iron road. They are coming nearer every day. There will be a time when you will mix with these people. That is when the Gray Eyes are going to get you to drink black, hot water, which you will drink whenever you eat. Then your teeth will become soft. They will get you to smoke at a young age, so that your eyes will run tears on windy days, and your eyesight will be poor. Your joints will crack when you want to move slowly and softly.

"You will sleep on soft beds and will not like to rise early. When you begin to wear heavy clothes and sleep under heavy covers, then you will grow lazy. Then there will be no more singing heard in the valleys as you walk.

"When you begin to eat with iron sticks, your tones will grow louder. You will speak louder and overtalk your parents. You will grow disobedient. Then when you mix with these gray-eyed people, you will learn their ways, you will break up homes, and murder and steal."

Such things have come true, and I compare my generation with the old generation. We are not as good as they were; neither are we healthy as they were.

How did these old men know what was coming? That is what I would like to know.

James Paytiamo
Acoma

INDIAN BOARDING SCHOOL

The school was a big change. Like sleeping on a good bed. And eating on a table, what we never did. We ate at home on the floor. So that was a great change. And bathing in a bathtub. We didn't have those things at home. Running water, you know. Anything inside. Anything we do, we go outside, or we carry our water in for bathing. So that was a lot of change. And the way they dressed us when we came down here, that was some change. They had to take [our Indian clothes] back because we weren't allowed to wear our own clothes.

Taos schoolgirl, circa 1919

PROPHECIES OF OUR GRANDPARENTS

Many years ago when our grandparents foresaw what our future would be like, they spoke their prophecies among themselves and passed them on to the children before them.

"Cities will progress and then decay to the ways of the lowest beings. Drinkers of dark liquids will come upon the land, speaking nonsense and filth. Then the end shall be nearer.

"Population will increase until the land can hold no more. The tribes of men will mix. The dark liquids they drink will cause the people to fight among themselves. Families will break up: father against children and children against one another.

"Maybe when the people have outdone themselves, then maybe, the stars will fall upon the land, or drops of hot water will rain upon the earth. Or the land will turn under. Or our father, the sun, will not rise to start the day. Then our possessions will turn into beasts and devour us whole.

"If not, there will be an odor from gases, which will fill the air we breathe, and the end for us shall come.

"But the people themselves will bring upon themselves what they receive. From what has resulted, time alone will tell what the future holds for us."

The Zuni people,
translated by Alvina Quam

BOARDING SCHOOL BLUES

I was a little girl. I remember it was in October and we had a pile of red chile and we were tying chile into fours. And then my grandfather was putting them onto a longer string. We were doing that when they came to get me. Then right away my grandma and my mother started to cry, "Her? She's just a little girl! You can't take her."

Tablita Woman Dancer,
San Ildefonso (1905)
Edward S. Curtis

I can still see my mother and my grandmother just crying their hearts out, wiping with their sleeves. They used to have full sleeves on their dresses that they made, and they were crying.

My mother put her best shawl on me. It was getting a little chilly. It was late. Pretty soon the train whistled around the bend near the Rio Grande, and it came. I was already five years old, but my grandpa was holding me on his lap, loving me. So when the train came, I got in. I saw the tears coming out of that brave man, my grandpa, who was so brave and strong.

I still picture my folks to this day, just standing there crying, and I was missing them. My grandfather, tears coming out of his eyes. I got on the train and I don't even know who was in the train because my mind was so full of unhappiness and sadness that I just don't know who was on that train at all.

San Juan schoolgirl, circa 1915

THE IMPORTANCE OF A SHAWL

That [Indian School] lady said she was taking my shawl off. She didn't want me to wear a shawl. You know, they didn't want us Indians to be Indians in those days. They want us to be something else than that. And she wanted to take my shawl. *No!* I held it to me because that shawl touched my mother and I loved it. I wanted it to touch me.

That first day, the adjutant took me downstairs. We had breakfast first. There were two restrooms with showers on one side, and then a long row of sinks. There were faucets. . . . She put me in the shower and told me to take a shower. She told me to wash my hair good. As she put me outside in the sun, she rubbed kerosene in my hair because I had nits and black bugs in my hair. In those days, there was hardly any water. We had to go far to get our water. Like I said, we go to the canal to bathe.

After my hair dried, they took me to the sewing room to be measured for my clothes. For nightgowns, two of everything. We had what they call bloomers. They were made out of denim. Thick denim, like you use for mattress covers. We had two school dresses, and two everyday dresses, and one uniform made out serge, and a cape. They measured me for all that.

From there she took me to the principal's office. I still had my shawl on because they could not make me take my shawl off. I kept holding it. I didn't want them to take my shawl. I put it back on as soon as she told me to dress and all.

The principal pointed to a clock up there and he asked me if I could tell the time. I just looked at it and I didn't know what to say. I didn't know how to tell time, so I just covered my face [with my shawl] and the students laughed.

Taos schoolgirl, circa 1915

HOW AN INDIAN LOOKS AT LIFE

I will come to you
And take you by the hand,
Let you walk with me in my paths,
The paths of moccasin footprints,
    in search of things,
    of my people I love.

We will call on the stars to guide us.
We will follow the music
    of the Fluteplayer in the air we breathe.
When we have reached those places of worship,
    these humble places
    where my ancestors once stood in silent prayer
I will try to explain the meaning
    of our beautiful prayers from the Old Ones.
And why my people are the way your eyes see them
And you sometimes cannot understand.
I would teach you names
    of Mother Earth's creatures and all her gifts.
I would share my moccasins with you
and let you walk my paths,
    my corn meal paths,
    my yellow pollen paths,
That you may know
And hear echoes of the past as I do.
Then you will know why it is not easy
    sometimes to be an Indian
And live as you do, my non–Indian friends.
You are also great people
    with much to learn
    much to give.
Together we will walk
    on this, Mother Earth's land,
    in peace with love
    and respect for each other
As only Mother Earth intended.

Lucy Lowden
Jemez

RIGHT OF WAY

The elder people at home do not understand.
It is hard to explain to them.
The questions from their mouths
and on their faces are unanswerable.
You tell them, "The State wants right of way.
It will get right of way."

They ask, "What is right of way?"
You say, "The State wants to go through
your land. The State wants your land."
They ask, "The Americans want my land?"
You say, "Yes, my beloved Grandfather."
They say, "I already gave them some land."
You say, "Yes, Grandmother, that's true.
Now, they want more, to widen their highway."
They ask again and again, "This right of way
that Americans want, does that mean
they want all our land?"

There is silence.
There is silence.
There is silence because you can't explain,
and you don't want to, and you know
when you use words like industry
and development and corporations
it wouldn't do any good.

There is silence.
There is silence.
You don't like to think
the fall into a bottomless despair
is too near and too easy and meaningless.
You don't want that silence to grow
deeper and deeper into you
because that growth inward stunts you,
and that is no way to continue,
and you want to continue.

And so you tell stories.
You tell stories about your People's birth
and their growing.
You tell stories about your children's birth
and their growing.
You tell the stories of their struggles.
You tell that kind of history,
and you pray and be humble.
With strength, it will continue that way.
That is the only way.
That is the only way.

Simon J. Ortiz
Acoma

OPPOSITE:
Flute Player (1939)
José Rey Toledo
Jemez

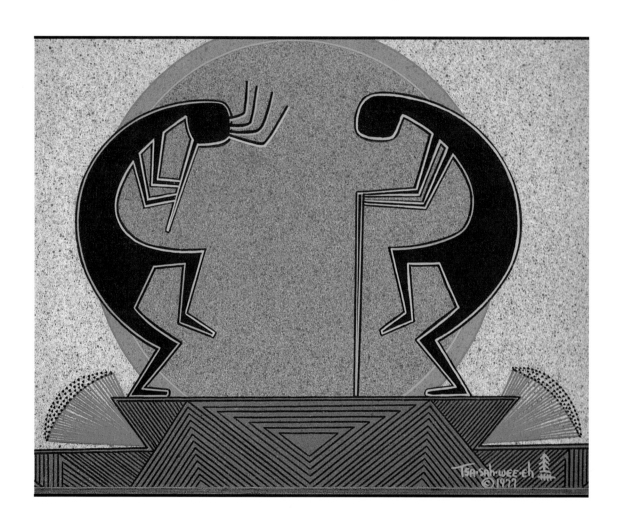

Humpback Flute Player
(1977)
Helen Hardin
Santa Clara

NOTES ON SELECTED CONTRIBUTORS

ALLEN, PAULA GUNN   Of Laguna/Sioux descent, Paula Gunn Allen is a respected scholar, feminist, and Indian advocate. She is the author of numerous critically acclaimed books, including *The Sacred Hoop* and *Skins and Bones*. She is a professor of English at UCLA.

AUSTIN, MARY   Feminist, mystic, amateur folklorist, and self-appointed champion of the Southwest Indian and the Spanish American, Mary Austin produced thirty-two books and more than two hundred essays. Her novel *Starry Adventure* (1931) is notable for the way in which the New Mexican landscape serves as the chief character of the story.

BANDELIER, ADOLF F.   One of the earliest American archaeologists, Adolf Bandelier was born in Switzerland, came to the United States as a boy, and spent years doing pioneering research among the Anasazi ruins of New Mexico. His most famous novel, *The Delight Makers* (1890), is a vivid account of prehistoric Indian life in the Southwest.

BOAS, FRANZ   A German-born American geographer, educator, linguist, anthropologist, editor, and author, Franz Boas is considered by many historians to be the founding father of American anthropology. His work among the Pueblos in the latter part of the nineteenth century laid the groundwork for in-depth twentienth-century study.

CATHER, WILLA   Virginia-born Willa Cather was awarded the Pulitzer Prize for fiction in 1923. Among her best-known novels is *Death Comes for the Archbishop*, a thinly veiled account of Bishop Jean-Baptiste Lamy of Santa Fe, who established a diocese in New Mexico in the mid-nineteenth century.

CLARK, ANN NOLAN   Ann Nolan Clark, a native New Mexican, worked for many years as an education specialist at the Bureau of Indian Affairs while writing a remarkable series of children's books on everyday life among the Pueblos, the Navajos, and the Sioux.

CONCHA, AGRIPITO   The cacique, or chief elder, of Taos Pueblo, Agripito "Pete" Concha was a leader in the fight to regain the tribe's sacred Blue Lake. His lifetime position is hereditary.

CONCHA, JOSEPH L.   While still a child at Taos Pueblo, Joseph Concha began to write poetry about his village and his people. Now in his forties, Mr. Concha is widely anthologized.

CURTIS, EDWARD S.   In a herculean body of work spanning nearly thirty years, Edward S. Curtis recorded the lives of the Indians of North America between 1904 and 1930, preserving in forty thousand photographs, ten thousand cylinder recordings, and millions of words the spirit, lives, and hardships of a changing culture. When he died in 1952, *The New York Times* devoted only seventy-five words to his obituary.

CUSHING, FRANK HAMILTON   The most controversial of all nineteenth-century anthropologists, Frank Cushing moved into a vacant house in Zuni Pueblo and extracted tribal secrets from the people during his four-and-a-half-year stay. In 1889, he was forced out and returned to Washington, D.C., where he wrote his books.

DOWNEY, VICKIE   Vickie Downey is an elder and a storyteller from Tesuque Pueblo.

ERDOES, RICHARD   Austrian-born artist, photographer, and writer Richard Erdoes has championed Indian causes for forty years, particularly those of the Lakota, whom he befriended in 1953. Mr. Erdoes has written extensively on the Pueblo Indians and compiled, with Alfonso Ortiz, a landmark collection of Indian tales, *American Indian Myths and Legends*.

ESPINOSA, CARMEN GERTRUDIS   A direct descendant of one of the original Spanish families that colonized New Mexico in the sixteenth century, Carmen Gertrudis Espinosa is past president of the New Mexico Folklore Society.

HARDIN, HELEN   A gifted Santa Clara painter who combined traditional with contemporary motifs, Helen Hardin spent her short life (1943–1984) experimenting with a new Pueblo Indian art form. She could neither abandon her heritage nor accept its inherent constraints. She is widely regarded as without peer in the field of contemporary Indian art.

HARRINGTON, JOHN P.   John Harrington was an often controversial ethnologist who, in 1918, gathered information from Picuris elder Rosendo Vargas for *Indian Tales from Picuris Pueblo*, one of his many books.

HILLERMAN, TONY   An internationally acclaimed author of more than a dozen mysteries set in the Navajo nation, Tony Hillerman has been, among other things, a journalist, a truck driver, and a professor. He has said that *The Boy Who Made Dragonfly* is his personal favorite of his many popular works.

HODGE, GENE MEANY   Gene Meany Hodge, an anthropologist, specialized in tales of the Kachinas, which she described as "lovable and kindly supernaturals who bring rain and other blessings."

HOTVEDT, KRIS   A noted artist with a strong commitment to Southwestern culture, Kris Hotvedt combines descriptive accounts of Pueblo events with striking woodcuts.

HOUSER, ALLAN   Often called the Henry Moore of Native American sculpture, Allan Houser won international acclaim for his bronzes, many of them larger than life-size. Mr. Houser, a Chiricahua Apache, drew heavily on his knowledge of mythology yet also incorporated the classic form and fluid lines of the masters. He died in 1994.

JAMES, AHLEE   An Eastern schoolteacher who traveled west in 1923 in search of adventure, Ahlee James settled in San Ildefonso and there, for the next three years, gathered unusual tribal tales and lore for *Tewa Firelight Tales* (1927).

LA FARGE, OLIVER   Best known as the author of *Laughing Boy*, which won the Pulitzer Prize for fiction in 1927, Oliver La Farge was a trained anthropologist who brought the insight of a writer to his many books about the Southwest.

LAWRENCE, D. H.   British novelist, poet, and essayist D. H. Lawrence wrote several groundbreaking novels, including *Sons and Lovers* and *Lady Chatterley's Lover*. He and his wife, Frieda, lived briefly in Taos, where his keen observations of Pueblo rituals resulted in several fine essays and pen-and-ink drawings.

LIGHTHALL, J. I.   A self-described "Indian medicine man," J. I. Lighthall roamed the continent in the 1870s, gathering Indian herbs and remedies and dispensing folksy wisdom.

LITTLEBIRD, HAROLD   Of Laguna and Santo Domingo heritage, Harold Littlebird is a noted storyteller, poet, and artist in the classic tradition.

LITTLEBIRD, LARRY   Larry Littlebird is the founder and director of Coyote Gathers His People, an educational organization based upon the Tribal American learning process and Pueblo Indian oral tradition. He is of Laguna and Santo Domingo descent.

LOPEZ, BARRY   Long recognized as a master storyteller, Barry Lopez, winner of the John Burroughs Society Medal for distinguished natural history writing for *Of Wolves and Men*, is one of America's leading voices for the values of the natural world.

LUMMIS, CHARLES F.   A pioneer ethnographer, author, and lecturer, Charles Lummis devoted his life to recording in text and photographs the Spanish and Indian songs, legends, and tales that he loved. He was the founder of the Southwest Museum in Los Angeles.

McNICKLE, D'ARCY   A Flathead Indian from Montana, D'Arcy McNickle wrote *Runner in the Sun*, a tale of Anasazi life in fourteenth-century New Mexico, rendered with astonishing vision and accuracy.

MIRABAL, ROBERT   Robert Mirabal, a Taos Indian, is among the younger generation of Indian writers who are presenting their culture in new and original terms. He also plays the flute professionally.

MOMADAY, N. SCOTT   One of America's best-known Native American writers, N. Scott Momaday, winner of the Pulitzer Prize for *House Made of Dawn*, draws on his Kiowa heritage for much of his fiction. He grew up at Jemez Pueblo, the setting of the novel. Mr. Momaday is also a professor and a gifted artist who has exhibited widely.

NARANJO-MORSE, NORA Known as a teacher of the techniques of Santa Clara Pueblo pottery throughout the American West, Denmark, and Germany, Nora Naranjo-Morse has exhibited her work in galleries all across the United States. She is a published poet as well.

ORTIZ, ALFONSO Alfonso Ortiz, a leading Native American anthropologist and professor at the University of New Mexico, wrote several major works, including *New Perspectives on the Pueblos*. A native of San Juan Pueblo, he was the editor, with William C. Sturtevant, of *Handbook of North American Indians, Volume 9: Southwest*, published by the Smithsonian Institution. He died in early 1997.

ORTIZ, SIMON J. Widely regarded as New Mexico's greatest Native American poet, Simon Ortiz conveys the hope and the vision of his cherished Acoma tribe. His book *Woven Stone* is a classic of Native American literature.

PEÑA, TONITA Tonita Peña, whose Indian name was Quah Ah, was born in 1893 at San Ildefonso. Raise at Cochiti, she was a renowned artist by the age of twenty-five, painting what she knew best—scenes of everyday life at the pueblo. She died in 1949.

PINO, MANUEL A member of the Acoma tribe, Manuel Pino is a journalist, storyteller, and the editor of *Americans Before Columbus*.

REED, EVELYN DAHL The wife of an anthropologist, Evelyn Reed acquired firsthand the Pueblo peoples' collected knowledge of the past and prehistory of the Southwest. One of her specialties was collecting coyote myths.

ROYBAL, ALFONSO *See* Tsireh, Awa.

SANDO, JOE S. Joe Sando, of Jemez Pueblo, is a historian, educator, scholar, and the author of *The Pueblo Indians*, an accurate and compelling history of New Mexico's Pueblos. Educated at Indian and mission schools, he later attended Eastern New Mexico College and Vanderbilt University. He is the recipient of numerous honors and awards.

SILKO, LESLIE MARMON Raised at Laguna Pueblo, Leslie Marmon Silko belongs to the new generation of Native American writers who combine tradition and love of place with the contemporary realities of hunger, poverty, and injustice. Her milestone works, *Ceremony* and *Storyteller*, established her as a major talent. She is the recipient of a MacArthur Foundation grant.

SWENTZELL, RINA Rina Swentzell, of Santa Clara Pueblo, is an architect and educator who has written extensively on the meaning behind Pueblo Indian architecture.

TSIREH, AWA Also known as Alfonso Roybal, Awa Tsireh was born about 1895 at San Ildefonso. His sublimely simple art is of several distinctive styles: semirealistic pictures; traditional paintings in the flat, two-dimensional style of San Ildefonso; and an abstract idiom.

TYLER, HAMILTON A. Hamilton Tyler, a passionate student of the Pueblo peoples, has written several major works, including *Pueblo Birds and Myths*, *Pueblo Gods and Myths*, and *Pueblo Animals and Myths*.

VALLO, LAWRENCE JONATHAN Of Jemez and Acoma descent, Lawrence Jonathan Vallo wrote and illustrated a slim volume called *Tales of a Pueblo Boy* that described what it was like to grow up as an Indian during the first part of this century.

VELARDE, PABLITA A native of Santa Clara Pueblo, artist Pablita Velarde, whose Indian name is Tse Tsan (Golden Dawn), has recently gained worldwide recognition for her powerful depictions of tribal legends.

WATERS, FRANK Considered by many to be the finest chronicler of the vast American Southwest, Frank Waters wrote more than twenty books during his lifetime, including the classic *The Man Who Killed the Deer*, *Masked Gods*, and *The Book of the Hopi*. He was nominated five times for the Nobel Prize in Literature.

WOOD, NANCY Poet, novelist, and photographer Nancy Wood has been involved with the Pueblo Indians for many years. Her books of poetry include *Spirit Walker*, *Many Winters*, and *Dancing Moons*.

SELECTED BIBLIOGRAPHY

Alexander, Hartley. *God's Drum and Other Cycles from Indian Lore*. New York: E. P. Dutton and Company, 1927.

Allen, Paula Gunn. *Grandmothers of the Light: A Medicine Woman's Sourcebook*. Boston: Beacon Press, 1991.

———. *Shadow Country*. Los Angeles: American Indian Studies Center, University of California, 1982.

———. *Women in American Indian Society*. New York: Chelsea House Publishers, 1992.

Anaya, Rudolfo, and Simon Ortiz. *Ceremony of Brotherhood*. Albuquerque: Academia, 1981.

Astrov, Margot, ed. *American Indian Prose and Poetry*. New York: Capricorn Books, 1962.

Austin, Mary. *The American Rhythm*. New York: Harcourt, Brace and Company, 1923.

———. *One-Smoke Stories*. Cambridge, Mass.: Houghton Mifflin Company, 1934.

Bandelier, Adolf F. *The Delight Makers*. New York: Dodd, Mead and Company, 1916.

Bierhorst, John, ed. *In the Trail of the Wind: American Indian Poems and Ritual Orations*. Toronto: Collins Publishers, 1971.

Boas, Franz, ed. *The Journal of American Folk-Lore* 31, no. 122.

Campbell, David. *Native American Folklore: A Cultural Celebration*. New York: Crescent Books, 1993.

Cather, Willa. *Death Comes for the Archbishop*. New York: Vintage Books, 1955.

Chavez, Tibo J. *New Mexican Folklore of the Rio Abajo*. Portales, N. Mex.: Bishop Printing Company, 1972.

Clark, Ann Nolan. *In My Mother's House*. New York: Puffin Books, 1992.

———. *Little Boy with Three Names: Stories of Taos Pueblo*. Santa Fe: Ancient City Press, 1990.

———. *Sun Journey: A Story of Zuni Pueblo*. Santa Fe: Ancient City Press, 1988.

Concha, Agripito. "The Bear." *New Mexico Magazine* (December 1994).

Concha, Joseph L. *Chokecherry Hunters and Other Poems*. Santa Fe: Sunstone Press, 1976.

———. *Lonely Deer: Poems by a Pueblo Indian Boy*. Taos. N. Mex.: Red Willow Society, 1969.

Cronyn, George W., ed. *American Indian Poetry*. New York: Ballantine Books, 1972.

Cushing, Frank Hamilton. *The Mythic World of the Zuni*. Albuquerque: University of New Mexico Press, 1988.

Downey, Vickie. *Wisdom's Daughters*. New York: HarperCollins Publishers, 1993.

Erdoes, Richard, and Alfonso Ortiz, eds. *American Indian Myths and Legends*. New York: Pantheon Books, 1984.

Espinosa, Carmen Gertrudis. *The Freeing of the Deer and Other New Mexico Indian Myths*. Albuquerque: University of New Mexico Press, 1985.

Fergusson, Erna. *Dancing Gods: Indian Ceremonials of New Mexico and Arizona*. Albuquerque: University of New Mexico Press, 1966.

Foss, Phillip, ed. *The Clouds Threw This Light: Contemporary Native American Poetry*. Santa Fe: American Indian Arts Press, 1983.

Gordon-McCutchan, R. C. *The Taos Indians and the Battle for Blue Lake*. Santa Fe: Red Crane Books, 1991.

Gray, Samuel L. *Tonita Peña*. Albuquerque: Avanyu Publishing, 1990.

Hall-Quest, Olga. *Conquistadors and Pueblos*. New York: E. P. Dutton and Company, 1969.

Harrington, John P., ed. *Indian Tales from Picuris Pueblo*. Santa Fe: Ancient City Press, 1989.

Hausman, Gerald, and Karl and Jane Kopp, eds. *Southwest: A Contemporary Anthology*. Albuquerque: Red Earth Press, 1977.

Hillerman, Tony. *The Boy Who Made Dragonfly*. Albuquerque: University of New Mexico Press, 1993.

———, ed. *The Spell of New Mexico*. Albuquerque: University of New Mexico Press, 1976.

Hobson, Geary. *The Remembered Earth: An Anthology of Contemporary Native American Literature*. Albuquerque: Red Earth Press, 1979.

Hodge, Gene Meany, ed. *Kachina Tales from the Indian Pueblos*. Santa Fe: Sunstone Press, 1993.

Hotvedt, Kris. *Pueblo and Navajo Indian Life Today*. Santa Fe: Sunstone Press, 1993.

Hughes, Phyllis, ed. *Pueblo Indian Cookbook: Recipes from the Pueblos of the American Southwest*. Albuquerque: Museum of New Mexico Press, 1977.

Hyer, Sally. *One House, One Heart: Native American Education at the Santa Fe Indian School*. Albuquerque: Museum of New Mexico Press, 1990.

Judson, Katharine Berry. *Myths and Legends of California and the Old Southwest*. Lincoln: University of Nebraska Press, 1994.

Keegan, Marcia. *Southwest Indian Cookbook*. Santa Fe: Clear Light Publishers, 1994.

La Farge, Oliver. *Yellow Sun, Bright Sky*. Albuquerque: University of New Mexico Press, 1988.

Lighthall, J. I. *Indian Folk Medicine Guide*. New York: Popular Library, not dated.

Littlebird, Harold. *On Mountains' Breath*. Santa Fe: Tooth of Time Books, 1982.

Lopez, Barry. *Giving Birth to Thunder, Sleeping with His Daughter: Coyote Builds North America*. New York: Avon Books, 1977.

Luhan, Mabel Dodge. *Winter in Taos*. New York: Harcourt, Brace and Company, 1935.

Lummis, Charles F. *Some Strange Corners of Our Country: The Wonderland of the Southwest*. New York: The Century Company, 1892.

Marriott, Alice, and Carol K. Rachlin. *American Indian Mythology*. New York: Harper & Row, Publishers, 1968.

McNickle, D'Arcy. *Runner in the Sun*. Philadelphia: The John C. Winston Company, 1954.

McNierney, Michael, ed. *Taos 1847: The Revolt in Contemporary Accounts*. Boulder, Colo: Johnson Publishing, 1989.

Miller, John. *Desert Light*. San Francisco: Chronicle Books, 1993.

Mirabal, Robert. *Skeleton of a Bridge*. Taos, N. Mex.: Blinking Yellow Books, 1994.

Momaday, N. Scott. *Circle of Wonder: A Native American Christmas Story*. Santa Fe: Clear Light Publishers, 1994.

———. *House Made of Dawn*. New York: Harper & Row, Publishers, 1966.

———. *The Way to Rainy Mountain*. Albuquerque: University of New Mexico Press, 1969.

Murphy, Charles J. *American Indian Corn (Maize)*. New York: G. P. Putnam's Sons, 1917.

Nabokov, Peter, ed. *Native American Testimony: A Chronicle of Indian-White Relations from Prophecy to the Present (1492–1992)*. New York: Penguin Books, 1978.

Naranjo-Morse, Nora. *Mud Woman: Poems from the Clay*. Tucson: University of Arizona Press, 1992.

Niethammer, Carolyn. *American Indian Food and Lore*. New York: Collier Macmillan Publishing Company, 1974.

Ortiz, Simon J. *The People Shall Continue*. Emeryville, Calif.: Children's Book Press, 1977.

———. *Woven Stone*. Tucson: University of Arizona Press, 1992.

Parsons, Elsie Clews. *Taos Tales*. Originally published by the American Folk–Lore Society, 1940. New York: Kraus Reprint Company, 1969.

Pijoan, Teresa. *White Wolf Woman and Other Native American Transformation Myths*. Little Rock, Ark.: August House, 1992.

Reed, Evelyn Dahl. *Coyote Tales from the Indian Pueblos*. Santa Fe: Sunstone Press, 1988.

Riley, Patricia. *Growing Up Native American*. New York: Avon Books, 1993.

Roman, Trish Fox. *Voices Under One Sky*. Nelson, Canada: The Crossing Press, 1994.

Rosen, Kenneth, ed. *The Man to Send Rain Clouds: Contemporary Stories by American Indians*. New York: Vintage Books, 1975.

Sando, Joe S. *The Pueblo Indians*. San Francisco: The Indian Historian Press, 1976.

Silko, Leslie Marmon. *Storyteller*. New York: Seaver Books, 1981.

Simmons, Marc. *Witchcraft in the Southwest: Spanish and Indian Supernaturalism on the Rio Grande*. Lincoln: University of Nebraska Press, 1974.

Spinden, Herbert Joseph, trans. *Songs of the Tewa*. Santa Fe: Sunstone Press, 1976.

Swentzell, Rina. "Remembering Tewa Pueblo Houses and Spaces," *Native Peoples: The Arts and Life-ways* 3, no. 2 (winter 1990).

Tyler, Hamilton A. *Pueblo Gods and Myths*. Norman: University of Oklahoma Press, 1986.

Vallo, Lawrence Jonathan. *Tales of a Pueblo Boy*. Santa Fe: Sunstone Press, 1987.

Waters, Frank. *The Man Who Killed the Deer*. Denver: Sage Books, 1942.

Weiner, Michael A. *Earth Medicine, Earth Food*. New York: Ballantine Books, 1979.

Witt, Shirley Hill, and Stan Steiner, eds. *The Way: An Anthology of American Indian Literature*. New York: Vintage Books, 1972.

Wood, Nancy. *Many Winters*. New York: Delacorte Press, 1974.

The Zuni People. *The Zunis: Self-Portrayals*. Alvina Quam, trans. Albuquerque: University of New Mexico Press, 1973.

LITERATURE SOURCES

"The People Shall Continue," by Simon J. Ortiz. From *The People Shall Continue* by Simon J. Ortiz. Copyright © 1988; original edition, copyright © 1977 by Children's Book Press. ▼ "He'-Mish Means People," Anonymous, Jemez State Monument. ▼ "The Coming of Corn," Zuni tale retold by Alice Marriott and Carol K. Rachlin. From *American Indian Mythology*. Copyright © 1968 by Alice Marriott and Carol K. Rachlin. Reprinted by permission of HarperCollins Publishers, Inc. ▼ "Making Bread from Corn Meal and Rye Flour," Traditional Pueblo recipe. From *American Indian Corn (Maize)* by Charles J. Murphy. Copyright © 1917 by Charles J. Murphy. ▼ "The Origin of Clans and Societies," Zuni tale retold by Frank Hamilton Cushing. From *The Mythic World of the Zuni* by Frank Hamilton Cushing. Copyright © 1988 by University of New Mexico Press. ▼ "The Dance of Life," by Nancy Wood. From *Many Winters*. Copyright © 1974 by Nancy Wood. ▼ "Spider's Creation," Zia legend retold by David Campbell. From *Native American Art and Folklore: A Cultural Celebration* by David Campbell. ▼ "The Great Flood," Zia tale retold by David Campbell. From *Native American Art and Folklore: A Cultural Celebration* by David Campbell. ▼ "The Pueblos by Language Groupings (1979)," by Joe S. Sando. ▼ "The Origin of the Morning Star," Zuni tale retold by Franz Boas. From *The Journal of American Folk-Lore*. ▼ "The Stars," by Pablita Velarde. From *Old Father Storyteller* by Pablita Velarde. Copyright © by Pablita Velarde. Reprinted by permission of Clear Light Publishers. ▼ "Taos Beaver Tail Roast," by Phyllis Hughes. From *Pueblo Indian Cookbook: Recipes from the Pueblos of the American Southwest*, compiled and edited by Phyllis Hughes. Copyright © 1977 by Museum of New Mexico Press. ▼ "The Unborn," by Hamilton A.

Tyler. From *Pueblo Gods and Myths* by Hamilton A. Tyler. Reprinted by permission of University of Oklahoma Press. Copyright © 1964 by the University of Oklahoma Press, Norman. ▼ "Prayer Spoken While Presenting an Infant to the Sun," Zuni tale retold by Margot Astrov. From *American Indian Prose and Poetry*, edited by Margot Astrov. ▼ "Song for the Newborn," Tewa tale retold by Mary Austin. From *The American Rhythm* by Mary Austin. Copyright © 1923, 1930 by Mary Austin. Copyright © renewed 1950 by Harry P. Mera, Kenneth M. Chapman, and Mary C. Wheelwright. Reprinted by permission of Houghton Mifflin Company. All rights reserved. ▼ "New Moon Daughter," by Harold Littlebird. From *On Mountains' Breath: Poetry and Drawings by Harold Littlebird*. Copyright © 1982 by Harold Littlebird. ▼ "The Little Girl and the Cricket," Tewa tale retold by Franz Boas. From *The Journal of American Folk-Lore*. ▼ "The Snake Who Ate Children," by Tonita Peña. From *Tonita Peña* by Samuel L. Gray. Copyright © 1990 by Avanyu Publishing, Inc. ▼ "Feeding the Spirits," by Pablita Velarde. From *Southwest Indian Cookbook* by Marcia Keegan. Copyright © 1987 Marcia Keegan. Reprinted by permission of Clear Light Publishers. ▼ "The Ghost," by the Zuni People, translated by Alvina Quam. From *The Zunis: Self-Portrayals* by the Zuni People. Copyright © 1972 by The Pueblo of Zuni. ▼ "Pueblo Christmas," by Lawrence Jonathan Vallo. From *Tales of a Pueblo Boy* by Lawrence Jonathan Vallo. Copyright © 1987 by Lawrence Jonathan Vallo. Reprinted by permission of Sunstone Press, Box 2321, Santa Fe, NM 87504. ▼ "Baby Eagles," Zuni tale retold by Ann Nolan Clark. Copyright © Ann Nolan Clark. From *Sun Journey: A Story of Zuni Pueblo*. Reprinted by permission of Ancient City Press. ▼ "Acoma and Laguna Calendar," by Hamilton A. Tyler. From *Pueblo Gods and Myths* by Hamilton A. Tyler. Copyright © 1964 by the University of Oklahoma Press. Reprinted by permission. ▼ "A Trick," by Larry Littlebird. From *Pueblo Gods and Myths*

by Hamilton A. Tyler. Copyright © 1964 by the University of Oklahoma Press. Reprinted by permission. ▼ "Have You Ever Hurt About Baskets?," by Marylita Altaka. From *Art and Indian Children*, No. 1, Curriculum Bulletin No. 7, Project Cultural Followthrough. ▼ "Circle of Wonder," by N. Scott Momaday. Originally titled "Native American Christmas Story," from *Circle of Wonder* by N. Scott Momaday. Copyright © 1994 by N. Scott Momaday. Reprinted by permission of Clear Light Publishers. ▼ "Instructions on Life," by Vickie Downey. From *Wisdom's Daughters: Conversations with Women Elders of Native America* by Steve Wall. Copyright © 1993 by Steve Wall. Reprinted by permission of Harper-Collins Publishers, Inc. ▼ "A Vast Old Religion" by D. H. Lawrence. From *The Spell of New Mexico*, edited by Tony Hillerman. ▼ "Pueblo Indian Religion," by Joe S. Sando. From *The Pueblo Indians* by Joe S. Sando. Copyright © 1976 by The Indian Historian Press, Inc. ▼ "All As It Was in This Place Timeless," by Nancy Wood. From *Hollering Sun* by Nancy Wood. Copyright © 1972 by Nancy Wood. ▼ "A Circle Begins," by Harold Littlebird. From *On Mountains' Breath: Poetry and Drawings by Harold Littlebird*. Copyright © 1982 by Harold Littlebird. ▼ "Going to Blue Lake," by Ann Nolan Clark. Copyright © Ann Nolan Clark. From *Little Boy with Three Names: Story of Taos Pueblo*. Reprinted by permission of Ancient City Press. ▼ "Spirit World of the Zunis," by the Zuni People, translated by Alvina Quam. From *The Zunis: Self-Portrayals* by the Zuni People. Copyright © 1972 by The Pueblo of Zuni. ▼ "Prayer to the Ancients After Harvesting," Zuni poem translated by Margot Astrov. From *American Indian Prose and Poetry*, edited by Margot Astrov. ▼ "The Pine Gum Baby," Santa Clara tale retold by Evelyn Dahl Reed. From *Coyote Tales from the Indian Pueblos*. Copyright © 1988 by Evelyn Dahl Reed. Reprinted by permission of Sunstone Press, Box 2321, Santa Fe, NM 87504. ▼ "Worshipping Water," by Pedro de Casteñeda. ▼ "Irrigation," by Ann Nolan Clark. From *In My Mother's House* by

Ann Nolan Clark. Copyright © 1941 by Ann Nolan Clark. Reprinted by permission of Viking Penguin, a division of Penguin Books USA Inc. ▼ "Rattlesnake Fools with Coyote," by Barry Lopez. From *Giving Birth to Thunder, Sleeping with His Daughter: Coyote Builds North America* by Barry Lopez. Copyright © 1977 by Barry Holstun Lopez. ▼ "On the Roof Throwing," Cochiti tale retold by Kris Hotvedt. From *Pueblo and Navajo Indian Life Today*. Copyright © 1993 by Kris Hotvedt. Reprinted by permission of Sunstone Press, Box 2321, Santa Fe, NM 87504. ▼ "The Harvesting of Corn Is Begun," by Carmen Gertrudis Espinosa. From *The Freeing of the Deer and Other New Mexico Indian Myths* by Carmen Gertrudis Espinosa. Copyright © 1985 by Carmen Gertrudis Espinosa. ▼ "Reminiscing With Pá-Pa (Grandmother) About Ka-tse-ma," by Manuel Pino. From *The Remembered Earth: An Anthology of Contemporary Native American Literature*, edited by Geary Hobson. ▼ "Famous Lost Words," by Pvt. Josiah M. Rice. From Pecos Pueblo Church, 1851. ▼ "A Woman Mourns for Her Husband," Zuni tale retold by Margot Astrov. From *American Indian Prose and Poetry*, edited by Margot Astrov. ▼ "Grandmother," by Joseph L. Concha. From *Chokecherry Hunters and Other Poems* by Joseph L. Concha. Copyright © 1976 by Joseph L. Concha. Reprinted by permission of Sunstone Press, Box 2321, Santa Fe, NM 87504. ▼ "Old Woman," by Nancy Wood. From *Many Winters* by Nancy Wood. Copyright © 1974 by Nancy Wood. ▼ "The Old Woman," Zuni tale retold by Tony Hillerman. From *The Boy Who Made Dragonfly* by Tony Hillerman. Reprinted by permission of Curtis Brown, Ltd. Copyright © 1972 by Tony Hillerman. ▼ "Sacred Shoes," by Paula Gunn Allen. From *Grandmothers of the Light: A Medicine Woman's Sourcebook* by Paula Gunn Allen. Copyright © 1991 by Paula Gunn Allen. Reprinted by permission of Beacon Press, Boston. ▼ "Now God Has Died," Santa Fe Municipal Council. ▼ "The Abode of Souls," Zuni tale retold by Frank Hamilton Cushing. From *The Mythic World of the Zuni* by Frank Hamilton Cushing. Copyright © 1988 by University of New Mexico Press. ▼ "How the Days Will Be," Zuni poem collected by John Bierhorst. From *In the Trail of the Wind: American Poems*

and Ritual Orations, edited by John Bierhorst. ▼ "The Borrowed Feathers," by Barry Lopez. From *Giving Birth to Thunder, Sleeping with His Daughter: Coyote Builds North America* by Barry Lopez. Copyright © 1977 by Barry Holstun Lopez. ▼ "The Origin of Death," Cochiti tale collected by Margot Astrov. From *American Indian Prose and Poetry*, edited by Margot Astrov. ▼ "Song of a Child's Spirit," Santo Domingo poem collected by Margot Astrov. From *American Indian Prose and Poetry*, edited by Margot Astrov. ▼ "A Very Good Day to Die," by Nancy Wood. From *Many Winters* by Nancy Wood. Copyright © 1974 by Nancy Wood. ▼ "Conquistador Hospitality, 1540," by Pedro de Casteñeda. ▼ "The Rock," by Willa Cather. From *Death Comes for the Archbishop* by Willa Cather. Copyright © 1929 by Willa Cather. Renewed 1957 by Edith Lewis and the City Bank Farmers Trust. Reprinted by permission of Alfred A. Knopf, Inc. ▼ "Anglo Intrusion," Anonymous, Jemez State Monument. ▼ "The Kiva," by D'Arcy McNickle. From *Runner in the Sun* by D'Arcy McNickle. Copyright © 1954 by D'Arcy McNickle. ▼ "Taos Pueblo, 1882," by Henry R. Poore. From *The Continent*, vol. 3, no. 61, April 11, 1883. ▼ "Oath of Office of the Pueblos," by Joe S. Sando. From *The Way: An Anthology of American Indian Literature*, edited by Shirley Hill Witt and Stan Steiner. Copyright © 1972 by Alfred A. Knopf, Inc. ▼ "The Ancient Strength," by Oliver La Farge. From *Yellow Sun, Bright Sky*. Reprinted by permission of Frances Collin Literary Agent. Copyright © 1988 by John Pendaries La Farge. ▼ "Remembering Tewa Pueblo Houses and Spaces," by Rina Swentzell. From *Native Peoples: The Arts and Lifeways*, vol. 3, no. 2, Winter 1990. Copyright © by Rina Swentzell. ▼ "A Snake Tale," San Juan tale retold by Edward S. Curtis. ▼ "A Fish Story," San Juan tale retold by Richard Erdoes and Alfonso Ortiz. From *American Indian Myths and Legends*, edited by Richard Erdoes and Alfonso Ortiz. Copyright © 1984 by Richard Erdoes and Alfonso Ortiz. ▼ "An Acoma Childhood," by Simon J. Ortiz. From *Growing Up Native American*, edited by Patricia Riley. ▼ "The Secret Trail," by D'Arcy McNickle. From *Runner in the Sun* by D'Arcy McNickle. Copyright © 1954 by D'Arcy McNickle. ▼ "The Man Who Killed the

Deer," by Frank Waters. From *The Man Who Killed the Deer* by Frank Waters. Copyright © by Frank Waters. ▼ "Hunter's Morning," by Harold Littlebird. From *On Mountains' Breath: Poetry and Drawings by Harold Littlebird*. Copyright © 1982 by Harold Littlebird. ▼ "The Deer Hunt," by Leslie Marmon Silko. Copyright © 1981 by Leslie Marmon Silko. Reprinted from *Storyteller* by Leslie Marmon Silko, published by Seaver Books, New York, New York. ▼ "How the Deer Got Their Red Eyes," Isleta tale collected by Gene Meany Hodge. From *Kachina Tales from the Indian Pueblos*, edited by Gene Meany Hodge. Reprinted by permission of Sunstone Press, Box 2321, Santa Fe, NM 87504. ▼ "The Rituals of Hunting," by the Zuni People, translated by Alvina Quam. From *The Zunis: Self-Portrayals* by the Zuni People. Copyright © 1972 by The Pueblo of Zuni. ▼ "Parched Corn," by Julia Roybal. From *Southwest Indian Cookbook* by Marcia Keegan. Copyright © 1987 by Marcia Keegan. Reprinted by permission of Clear Light Publishers. ▼ "Animal Dance," by Pablita Velarde. From *Southwest Indian Cookbook* by Marcia Keegan. Copyright © 1987 by Marcia Keegan. Reprinted by permission of Clear Light Publishers. ▼ "The Hunting Prayer," by Larry Littlebird. From *Hunting Sacred—Everything Listens: A Pueblo Indian Man's Legacy, Song, Story and Art from Oral Tradition*. Copyright © 1990 by Larry Littlebird. ▼ "When I Was Thirteen," by Leslie Marmon Silko. Copyright © 1981 by Leslie Marmon Silko. Reprinted from *Storyteller* by Leslie Marmon Silko, published by Seaver Books, New York, New York. ▼ "The Bear," by Agripito Concha. From *New Mexico Magazine*, December 1994. ▼ "Hunting," by Nancy Wood. From *Many Winters* by Nancy Wood. Copyright © 1974 by Nancy Wood. ▼ "Rabbit Hunt," by Robert Mirabal. From *Skeleton of a Bridge* by Robert Mirabal. Reprinted by permission of Blinking Yellow Books. ▼ "The Prairie Dogs Dance," Cochiti tale retold by Evelyn Dahl Reed. From *Coyote Tales from the Indian Pueblos* by Evelyn Dahl Reed. Copyright © 1988 by Evelyn Dahl Reed. Reprinted by permission of Sunstone Press, Box 2321, Santa Fe, NM 87504. ▼ "The Priest's Son and the Eagle," Zuni tale retold by Frank Hamilton Cushing. From *My Adventures in Zuñi* by Frank Hamilton Cushing. ▼ "A Sure Cure for Bots," by J. I. Lighthall. From *The Indian Folk Medicine Guide* by J. I. Lighthall. ▼ "Imprisoned by Bears," a Tewa tale retold by Ahlee James. From *Tewa Firelight Tales*, collected by Ahlee James. ▼ "The Importance of Cigarettes," by Charles F. Lummis. From *Some Strange Corners of Our Country: The Wonderland of the Southwest* by Charles F. Lummis. ▼ "Oh Sweet Her," by Joseph L. Concha. From *Chokecherry Hunters and Other Poems* by Joseph L. Concha. Copyright © 1976 by Joseph L. Concha. Reprinted by permission of Sunstone Press, Box 2321, Santa Fe, NM 87504. ▼ "Deer Hunter and White Corn Maiden," Tewa tale translated by Alfonso Ortiz. From *American Indian Myths and Legends*, edited by Richard Erdoes and Alfonso Ortiz. ▼ "The Sphynx Moth and the Old Coyote," Picuris tale retold by John P. Harrington. Copyright © John P. Harrington. From *Indian Tales from Picuris Pueblo*, edited by Marta Weigle. Reprinted by permission of Ancient City Press. ▼ "The Watermelon Race," by Carmen Gertrudis Espinosa. From *The Freeing of the Deer and Other New Mexico Indian Myths* by Carmen Gertrudis Espinosa. Copyright © 1985 by Carmen Gertrudis Espinosa. ▼ "The Delight Makers," by Adolf F. Bandelier. From *The Delight Makers* by Adolf F. Bandelier. ▼ "Antidote for Tobacco," by J. I. Lighthall. From *The Indian Folk Medicine Guide* by J. I. Lighthall. ▼ "The Snakes of Tesuque, 1924," by Edward S. Curtis. ▼ "Witchcraft," by Marc Simmons. Reprinted from *Witchcraft in the Southwest: Spanish and Indian Supernaturalism on the Rio Grande* by Marc Simmons. Copyright © 1974 by Marc Simmons. Reprinted by permission of the University of Nebraska Press. ▼ "Magpie Drowns Blue Corn Girl," Taos tale retold by Elsie Clews

Parsons. From *Taos Tales* by Elsie Clews Parsons. ▼ "True Way of the Scalp Dance," by the Zuni People, translated by Alvina Quam. From *The Zunis: Self-Portrayals* by the Zuni People. Copyright © 1972 by The Pueblo of Zuni. ▼ "San Geronimo," by Frank Waters. From *The Man Who Killed the Deer* by Frank Waters. Copyright © by Frank Waters. ▼ "Pueblo Reality," Anonymous Taos elder, retold by Nancy Wood. From *Many Winters* by Nancy Wood. Copyright © 1974 by Nancy Wood. ▼ "Kopis'taya (A Gathering of Spirits)," by Paula Gunn Allen. From *Grandmothers of the Light: A Medicine Woman's Sourcebook* by Paula Gunn Allen. Copyright © 1991 by Paula Gunn Allen. Reprinted by permission of Beacon Press, Boston. ▼ "Pecos Warriors at Jemez," by N. Scott Momaday. From *House Made of Dawn* by N. Scott Momaday. Copyright © 1966, 1967, 1968 by N. Scott Momaday. Reprinted by permission of HarperCollins Publishers, Inc. ▼ "The Pueblo Indians," by Joe S. Sando. From *The Pueblo Indians* by Joe S. Sando. Copyright © 1976 by The Indian Historian Press, Inc. ▼ "He Is Not One of Us," by Sun Elk. From *Native American Testimony: A Chronicle of Indian-White Relations from Prophecy to the Present, 1492–1992*, edited by Peter Nabokov. Copyright © Peter Nabokov, 1978, 1991. ▼ "My Great-Grandmother," by Leslie Marmon Silko. From *Storyteller* by Leslie Marmon Silko. Copyright © 1981 by Leslie Marmon Silko. Reprinted from *Storyteller* by Leslie Marmon Silko, published by Seaver Books, New York, New York. ▼ "Towa," by Nora Naranjo-Morse. From *Mud Woman: Poems from the Clay* by Nora Naranjo-Morse. Copyright © 1992 by the University of Arizona Press. ▼ "Echo from Beyond," by Joe S. Sando. From *The Remembered Earth: An Anthol-*

ogy of Contemporary Native American Literature, edited by Geary Hobson. Copyright © 1979 by Red Earth Press. ▼ "Mixed Blood," by Mary Austin. From *One-Smoke Stories* by Mary Austin. Copyright © 1934 by Mary Austin, © renewed 1961 by School of American Research. Reprinted by permission of Houghton Mifflin Company. All rights reserved. ▼ "Clay," by Rina Swentzell. From *Native Peoples: The Arts and Lifeways*, vol. 3, no. 2, Winter 1990. Copyright © by Rina Swentzell. ▼ "Religion," Anonymous, Jemez State Monument. ▼ "Easy Life of the Gray-Eyed," by James Paytiamo. From *Native American Testimony: An Anthology of Indian and White Relations: First Encounter to Dispossession*, edited by Peter Nabokov. ▼ "Indian Boarding School," by Taos schoolgirl. From *One House, One Voice, One Heart: Native American Education at the Santa Fe Indian School*, edited by Sally Hyer. Copyright © 1990 by Santa Fe Indian School. ▼ "Prophecies of Our Grandparents," by the Zuni People, translated by Alvina Quam. From *The Zunis: Self-Portrayals* by the Zuni People. Copyright © 1972 by The Pueblo of Zuni. ▼ "Boarding School Blues," by San Juan schoolgirl. From *One House, One Voice, One Heart: Native American Education at the Santa Fe Indian School*, edited by Sally Hyer. Copyright © 1990 by Santa Fe Indian School. ▼ "The Importance of a Shawl," by Taos schoolgirl. From *One House, One Voice, One Heart: Native American Education at the Santa Fe Indian School*, edited by Sally Hyer. Copyright © 1990 by Santa Fe Indian School. ▼ "How an Indian Looks at Life," by Lucy Lowden. From Jemez State Monument. ▼ "Right of Way," by Simon J. Ortiz. From *Woven Stone* by Simon J. Ortiz. Reprinted by permission of the author.

ART SOURCES

Horse in the Wind, by Ian Carlisle. Copyright © Ian Carlisle, from *Where There Is No Name for Art* by Bruce Hucko, School of American Research Press, Santa Fe, NM, 1996. ▼ *Emergence of the Corn Dance Clan*, by Robert Montoya. Courtesy of Indian Pueblo Cultural Center Museum. ▼ *Cleaning Wheat, San Juan*, photo by Edward S. Curtis. Courtesy of Museum of New Mexico. Negative number 144548. ▼ *Tyo'o'hi Shiwanna Mask, Cochiti*, photo by Edward S. Curtis. Courtesy of Museum of New Mexico. ▼ "Taos turtle dance," by Vincent Mirabal. Courtesy of Indian Arts and Crafts Board, U.S. Department of the Interior. ▼ *Dreams of Mimbres Fishermen*, by Helen Hardin. Copyright © Helen Hardin 1982. Photo copyright © 1997 by Cradoc Bagshaw. ▼ *Zuni Water Carriers*, photo by Edward S. Curtis. Courtesy of Museum of New Mexico. Negative number 76957. ▼ *Return from the Deer Hunt*, by Louis Naranjo. Photo by Mark Nohl. From *Indians of New Mexico*. Copyright © 1990 by *New Mexico Magazine*. ▼ *The Heart of Ohkay Owingeh*, by Daniel Archuleta. Copyright © Daniel Archuleta. From *Where There Is No Name for Art* by Bruce Hucko, School of American Research Press, Santa Fe, NM, 1996. ▼ *Coyote*, by Quincy Tafoya. Copyright © Quincy Tafoya. From *Where There Is No Name for Art* by Bruce Hucko, School of American Research Press, Santa Fe, NM, 1996. ▼ "Blessing of the newborn," by Harold Littlebird. From *On Mountains' Breath: Poetry and Drawings by Harold Littlebird*. Copyright © 1982 by Harold Littlebird. ▼ *A Taos Girl*, photo by Edward S. Curtis. Courtesy of Museum of New Mexico. Negative number 143738. ▼ "Killing the serpent," by José A. Martinez. Courtesy of School of American Research. Catalog Number IAF.P147. ▼ *Tsle-ka (Douglas Spruce Leaf), Cacique of San Juan*, photo by Edward S. Curtis. Courtesy of Museum of New Mexico. Negative number 144529. ▼ *The Demon of Childhood*, by Farny. From *My Adventures in Zuñi* by Frank Hamilton Cushing. ▼ *Santo Domingo Corn Dance*, reproduction by Mary Alice Schively, 1930. Courtesy of Museum of

Indian Arts and Culture/Laboratory of Anthropology, Santa Fe, NM. Catalog number 52129/13. ▼ *A Zuni Man*, photo by Edward S. Curtis. Courtesy of Museum of New Mexico. Negative number 143712. ▼ *Eagle Dancer, San Ildefonso*, photo by Edward S. Curtis. Courtesy Museum of New Mexico. ▼ *Okuwa-T'sire (Cloud Bird), San Ildefonso*, photo by Edward S. Curtis. Courtesy of Museum of New Mexico, Negative number 143728. ▼ *Pueblo Indian Dancers*, by D. H. Lawrence. From *Laughing Horse*, edited by Willard Johnson. Copyright © 1927 by Viking Press. ▼ *Runaway Koshare*, by José Rey Toledo, 1937. Courtesy of Museum of Indian Arts and Culture/Laboratory of Anthropology, Santa Fe, NM. Catalog number 51444/13. ▼ *Five Brothers*, by Jordan Harvier. Copyright © Jordan Harvier. From *Where There Is No Name for Art* by Bruce Hucko, School of American Research Press, Santa Fe, NM, 1996. ▼ *Rain Pond*, by Danielle Martinez. Copyright © Danielle Martinez. From *Where There Is No Name for Art* by Bruce Hucko, School of American Research Press, Santa Fe, NM, 1996. ▼ "Untitled (Taos)," by Ellison Hoover. Courtesy of the University of New Mexico Art Museum; museum purchase. ▼ *Zuni Planting*, by W. J. Metcalf. From *My Adventures in Zuñi* by Frank Hamilton Cushing. ▼ *Oyegi-a'Ye (Frost Moving)*, photo by Edward S. Curtis. Courtesy of Museum of New Mexico. Negative number 143721. ▼ "Tanning the hide" (untitled), by Alfonso Roybal (Awa Tsireh), © 1922. Courtesy of Museum of Indian Arts and Culture/Laboratory of Anthropology, Santa Fe, NM. Catalog number 24221/13. ▼ "Cleaning the ditch," by Joe Evan Duran (Po-re Pien), 1937. Courtesy of Museum of Indian Arts and Culture/Laboratory of Anthropology, Santa Fe, NM. Catalog number 53938/13. ▼ *Rainbow Pueblo*, by Eliza Morse. Copyright © Eliza Morse. From *Where There Is No Name for Art* by Bruce Hucko, School of American Research Press, Santa Fe, NM, 1996. ▼ *Sia War Dancer*, photo by Edward S. Curtis. Courtesy of Museum of New Mexico. ▼ *Iahla (Willow) Taos*, photo by

Edward S. Curtis. Courtesy of Museum of New Mexico. Negative number 143741. ▼ *Ancient Ancestors*, by Lee Moquino. Copyright © Lee Moquino. From *Where There Is No Name for Art* by Bruce Hucko, School of American Research Press, Santa Fe, NM, 1996. ▼ *Santana Quitana, Cochiti*, photo by Edward S. Curtis. Courtesy of Museum of New Mexico. ▼ *Wahu Toya, Pecos, at Jemez*, photo by John K. Hillers. Courtesy of Museum of New Mexico. Negative number 2604. ▼ "Buck and three coyotes," by Ascención H. Galvan. Courtesy of School of American Research Collections in the Museum of New Mexico, Santa Fe, NM. Catalog number 24051/13. ▼ *Conquistadores, 1540*, by Anders John Haugseth. From *God's Drum* by Hartley Alexander. Copyright © 1927 by E. P. Dutton. ▼ *Zuwang, Pecos, at Taos*, photo by Kenneth Chapman. Courtesy of Museum of New Mexico. Negative number 28318. ▼ *Cliff-perched Acoma*, photo by Edward S. Curtis. Courtesy of Museum of New Mexico. Negative number 144527. ▼ *Harvest Dance*, by J. D. Roybal. Courtesy of Indian Pueblo Cultural Center Museum. ▼ *A Taos Pet*, by Peter Moran. From *The Continent*. ▼ *A Narrow Street, Laguna*, photo by Edward S. Curtis. Courtesy Museum of New Mexico. Negative number 144715. ▼ *A San Juan Farmhouse*, photo by Edward S. Curtis. Courtesy of Museum of New Mexico. Negative number 144540. ▼ "Woman baking bread," by Awa Tsireh. Courtesy of School of American Research. Catalog number IAF.P16. ▼ *Mo'wa' (Shining Light), Nambe*, photo by Edward S. Curtis. Courtesy of Museum of New Mexico. Negative number 144513. ▼ *A Threshing-Floor at Taos Pueblo*, by Henry R. Poore. From *The Continent*. ▼ "Buffalo hunt," by José Rey Toledo. Courtesy of Indian Pueblo Cultural Center Museum. ▼ "The secret trail," by Allan Houser. From *Runner in the Sun* by D'Arcy McNickle. ▼ *The Old-Fashioned Deer Hunter*, by Ralph Martinez. Courtesy of School of American Research. Catalog number IAF.P196. ▼ "Hunting the deer," by Emiliana Yepa, 1937. Courtesy of Museum of Indian Arts and Culture/

Laboratory of Anthropology, Santa Fe, NM. Catalog number 51802/13. ▼ *Pecos Bull*, by Augustine Fragua. Courtesy of Museum of Indian Arts and Culture/Laboratory of Anthropology, Santa Fe, NM. Catalog number 24036/13. ▼ "Buffalo hunt," artist unknown. Courtesy of School of American Research. Catalog number SAR.P14. ▼ *Holy Deer*, by Larry Littlebird. From *Hunting Sacred—Everything Listens: A Pueblo Indian Man's Legacy, Song, Story and Art from Oral Tradition* by Larry Littlebird. Courtesy of Hunting Sacred Art Collection, Santa Fe, NM. Copyright © 1995 by Larry Littlebird. ▼ *Bear and Deer*, by Justino Herrera. Courtesy of Museum of Indian Arts and Culture/Laboratory of Anthropology, Santa Fe, NM. Catalog number 35392/13. ▼ *The Rabbit Hunter*, by Oscar Berninghaus. Collection of the Museum of Fine Arts, Museum of New Mexico. Given in memory of Maurice M. Mikesell by John A. and Margaret Hill. ▼ *Mountain Sheep Chasing the Koshare*, by Awa Tsireh, 1951. Courtesy of Museum of Indian Arts and Culture/Laboratory of Anthropology, Santa Fe, NM. Catalog number 35372/13. ▼ "Bear and paw prints," artist unknown. Courtesy of School of American Research. Catalog number SAR.1984–15–3. ▼ *Acoma Birds*, by Helen Hardin. Copyright © Helen Hardin 1977. Photo copyright © 1997 by Cardoc Bagshaw. ▼ *Sotsona (Fox), Santo Domingo*, photo by Edward S. Curtis. Courtesy of Museum of New Mexico. ▼ *Watermelon Break*, by Helen Hardin. Copyright © Helen Hardin 1978. Photo copyright © 1997 by Cradoc Bagshaw. ▼ *Woman Making Piki Bread*, by R. Joesyesva. Courtesy of Indian Arts and Culture/Laboratory of Anthropology, Santa Fe, NM. Catalog number 52705/13. ▼ *Prayer for Rain*, by Marcellus Medina. Courtesy of Indian Pueblo Cultural Center Museum. ▼ *Torturing a Sorcerer*, by Farny. From *My Adventures in Zuñi* by Frank Hamilton Cushing. ▼ *Dressing Young Girl for First Ceremonial*, by Pablita Velarde (Tse Tsan), 1939. Courtesy of School of American Research Collections in the Museum of New Mexico, Santa Fe, NM. Catalog number 24355/13. ▼ *Koshare*, by Rose M. Gachupin, ca. 1962. Courtesy of Museum of Indian Arts and Culture/Laboratory of Anthropology, Santa Fe, NM. Catalog number 35379/13. ▼ "Buffalo dancers," artist unknown. Courtesy of School of American Research. Catalog number SAR.1981–2–1. ▼ "Marie and blond tourist viewing pottery," by Gilbert Atencio, 1945. Courtesy of Museum of Indian Arts and Culture/Laboratory of Anthropology, Santa Fe, NM. Catalog number 24146/13. ▼ *Walvia (Medicine Root), Taos*, photo by Edward S. Curtis. Courtesy of Museum of New Mexico. Negative number 144536. ▼ *Female Harvest Corn Dance*, by Gilbert Atencio. Courtesy of Indian Pueblo Cultural Center Museum. ▼ *Zia Pueblo Potter*, by Velino Shije Herrara. Courtesy of School of American Research Collections in the Museum of New Mexico, Santa Fe, NM. Catalog number 35468/13. ▼ *Looking East*, by Kimberly Sisneros. Copyright © Kimberly Sisneros. From *Where There Is No Name for Art* by Bruce Hucko, School of American Research Press, Santa Fe, NM, 1996. ▼ *Tablita Woman Dancer, San Ildefonso*, photo by Edward S. Curtis. Courtesy Museum of New Mexico. Negative number 144546. ▼ *Flute Player*, by José Rey Toledo. Courtesy of Indian Pueblo Cultural Center Museum. ▼ *Humpback Flute Player*, by Helen Hardin. Copyright © Helen Hardin 1977.

INDEX

ML

2/02